Anonymous

Gems of German Song

A collection of the most beautiful vocal composition: with accompaniment for the

piano-forte

Anonymous

Gems of German Song
A collection of the most beautiful vocal composition: with accompaniment for the piano-forte

ISBN/EAN: 9783744795975

Printed in Europe, USA, Canada, Australia, Japan

Cover: Foto ©Thomas Meinert / pixelio.de

More available books at **www.hansebooks.com**

GEMS

OF

GERMAN SONG:

A COLLECTION OF THE MOST

BEAUTIFUL VOCAL COMPOSITIONS,

OF

BEETHOVEN, VON WEBER, MENDELSSOHN, SCHUBERT, ABT, KÜCKEN,

GUMBERT, KREBS, REICHARDT, SPOHR, PROCH, KELLER, ETC.

WITH ACCOMPANIMENT FOR THE

PIANO·FORTE.

BOSTON:
Published by OLIVER DITSON & CO., 277 Washington Street.
NEW YORK: C. H. DITSON & CO.

CONTENTS.

TO MINONA.

(SERENADE.)

Spohr.

Andantino.

1. Soft and low I breathe my pas - - sion, Will she
   smile, my love dis - dain - - ing, While in
   love, o'er plain and riv - - er, Late I
   not in dark - ness pi - - ning, From thy

wake and bless my sight; Ah! if dreams her form might
chill - - - ing mid - night's spite. Here I wait, of thee com -
rush'd in head - long flight; Ah! he fol - - low'd ev - - er,
our - - - tain'd win - dow's height Let one look of pi - ty

fash - ion. How un - wel - - come were the light; Fair - est, speak, and say good
p'ain - ing, To the stars so cold and bright; O! ro - lent, and say good
ev - - er, Vain is speed a - gainst his might; Here I yield, O! one good
shi - ning, Warm my heart to new de - light; Let me hear one sweet good

night!
night!
night!

2. Dost thou
3. Far from
4. Leave me

THE WANDERER.

F. Schubert.

From countries far a-way I come,
Ich kom-me vom Ge-bir-ge her,

Where'er I go,
es dampft das Thal,

Where'er I
es braust das

go,
Meer,
I find no home.
braust das Meer.

I wan - der on, de - void of peace,
Ich wand - le still, bin we - - - nig froh,

pp

Marcato.

My joys di - min - - ish, woes..... in - crease, woes..... in - - - - mer
Und im - - - - mer fragt der Seuf - - zer wo? im - - - - mer

p

ppp

- crease The sun's warm rays to me feel cold. My life's young days seem grow-ing old; The
wo! Die Son - ne dünkt mich hier so kalt, die Blü - the welk, das Le - ben alt, und

pp

bloom - ing flow - ers dead.... and sere, I feel a stran - ger ev' - ry - where.
was sie re - den los - - - rer Schall; ich bin ein Fremd - ling ü - - ber - all.

Cres.

pp

Più vivo.

Where art thou? where art thou? my be-lov-ed home. I turn,
Wo bist du, wo bist du, mein ge-lieb-tes Land! ge-sucht,

mf

Viva.

thee, where - e'er I roam, It
ahnt, und nie ge-kannt. Das

p   pp   fp

makes my ve-ry heart ex-pand, my heart ex-pand, To think of thee, my
Land, das Land so hoff-nungs-grün, so hoff-nungs-grün, das Land, wo mei-ne

f   p

na-tive land, Thy cliffs so white, thy hills so blue, Where blooms the rose and li-ly too, And
ro-sen blühn, wo mei-ne Freun-de wan-deln gehn, wo mei-ne Tod-ten auf-ersteh'n, das

Tempo primo.

ear - ly friends with hearts so true. Oh! land .... where art thou?
Land, das mei - ne Spra - che spricht, o Land .... wo bist du?

A spir - it's warn - - ing voice I hear, It whis - pers
Ich wand' - le still, bin we - nig froh. Und im - - - mer

soft - ly in .... my ear, in .... my ear, Soon shalt thou quit life's
fragt der Seuf - - zer wo? im - - - mer wo? Im Geis - ter - hauch tönt's

troubled wave, And find thy home in the si - lent grave.
mir zu - rück: Dort wo du nicht bist, dort ist das Glück.

Colla voce.

I WOULD THAT MY LOVE.

Mendelssohn

I would that my love could si - lent - ly flow in a single

thee . . . on their wings, my fair - est, that soul - felt word they would

word, I'd give it the mer - ry breez - es, They'd waft it away in

bear, Should'st hear it at eve - ry mo - ment, And hear . . . . it eve - ry

sport, I'd give it the mer - ry breez - es, they'd waft it a - way in

where, Should'st hear it at eve - ry mo - ment, and hear it eve - ry

sport, away in sport, they'd waft it away in sport.
and every where. and hear it eve-ry where.
where, a-way in sport, they'd waft it away in sport.
and eve-ry where, and hear it every where.
sf
sf
1st.
2nd.
To At night . when thine eyelids in
To At night . . when thine eyelids in
pp
pp
pp
slum - ber have clos'd those bright heav'nly beams, Still there my love it will
slum - ber have clos'd those bright heav'nly beams, Still there my love it will
Sempre.
pp
Cresc.

haunt thee e'en in thy deepest dreams, Still there my love it will

haunt thee e'en in thy deepest dreams, Still there my love it will

haunt thee e'en in .... thy deepest dreams, e'en in thy deep - est

haunt thee e'en in .... thy deepest dreams, thy deepest

E'en in ..... thy deepest, deep - est dreams.

dreams, E'en in ..... thy deepest, deep - est dreams.

MY JOY AND TREASURE.

(HERZALLERLIEBSTES SCHATZERL DU.)

Fr. Kücken.

Andantino.

1. Thou, who my treasure e'er shall be, Quick lock thy heart to
Herz - al - ler - lieb - stes Schat-zerl du, schliess schnell dein Herzen-
2. Come lit - tle treasure, joy to me, Clos'd to all else, thy

all but me, Thou art so fair, That oth - ers fain would en - ter there, there, La,
kam - merl zu, du bist so schön, 's mocht ein And' - rer zu dir geh'n. geh'n. La,
heart must be. Thou art, &c.

Dim.

Allegro.

La la la la la la la la la la la la la la la la la la la la la la la

la la la la la la la la la la la la la la la la la la la la la la la la   la la la   la la la la la la la la   la la   la la la....

Tempo 1o.

Thou who my treasure e'er shall be, Quick close thy heart to all but me, Thou art so
Herz al - ler - lieb - stes Schat - zerl du, schliess schnell dein Her - zens kam - merl zu, du bist so

dim. riten.

fair, That ma - ny fain would en - ter there.   Lov - ing thee is joy to me, but, O my love
schön, 's möcht ein And' - rer zu dir geh'n.   Dich zu lie - ben, giebt mir Frie - den, o meine
Thou my trea - sure and my joy, but, O my love
Dich um - fan - gen, mein Ver - lan - gen, o meine

Allegro. playful.   Tempo 1o des Trio.

and my pride, All else should be de - nied,   Lov - ing thee is joy to me.
Se - lig - keit, mach mir nicht Her - ze - leid,   Dich zu lie - ben, giebt mir Friede
and my pride, All else should be de - nied,   Thou my trea - sure and my joy,
Se - lig - keit, mach mir nicht Her - ze - leid.   Dich um - fan - gen, mein Ver - lan - gen

Yes, thou art mine, yes, thou art mine! 3. Come, lit - tle treasure, joy to me, Clos'd to all else, thy
ja, du bist mein, ja! du bist mein! Herz - al - ler - lieb - stes Schat - zerl du, schliess schnell dein Herzens-

heart must be. Thou art so fair, an - oth - er, dear, might en - ter there. Thou art so
kam - merl zu, du bist so schön, 's mocht ein And - rer zu dir geh'n. Du bist so

fair,...... so sweet and fair,.... thou art so fair,.... others fain would en - ter
schön ..... du bist so schön, ... du bist so schön, ... 's konnt' ein And'rer zu dir

there, thou art so fair, thou art so fair,............. so fair......
geh'n, du bist so schön, du bist so schön, ... so schön. ...

PRETTY BIRDS.

(O BITT' EUCH, LIEBE VÖGELEIN.)

English words by W. J. Wetmore, M. D.   Music by Ferd. Gumbert.

1. In greenwoods, where soft breez-es spring, Are hap-py birds that sweet-ly
1. Wohl vie-le tau-send Vö-ge-lein, die sin-gen hell im grü-nen
   vales where ro-ses fair, With perfume scent the balm-y
   sen-den in ein Thal, mit lust'gen Quel-len oh-ne

sing; O'er land and sea they swift-er fly, Than summer gales o'er flow'rs that
Hain, sie ha-ben all zwei Flü-gel-ein, sie flie-gen ü-ber Land und
air; There would I fly to love's sweet bow'rs, A gar-den sweet of bloom-ing
Zahl, da blü-hen Blu-men, süss und lind, und nei-gen sich in A-bend-

sigh; They soar a-way on pin-ions light, Their love tales war-bling in.... their
See'n, sie ha-ben al-le rü-s-sen Mund, Her-zens
flow'rs; There like a dream-land fair... and bright, Each ris-ing view adds new... de-
-wind, ich will euch sen-den vor... ein Haus da lacht der Früh-ling selbst... her-

Andante Con Molto Express.

flight. Come pret - - - ty birds, so glad . . . . and free, Oh
gruud. O bitt' euch lie . . . . . be Vö . . . ge - lein, O
- light. Come pret - - - ty birds, so glad . . . . and free,
- aus, O, &c.

let . . . . . . me still more hap - - py be, And bear my vows . . . . . . sin
bitt' euch lie - - - be Vö - ge - lein, will keins, will keins . . . . von

Legato.

- cere . . . . To her I love, I love so dear.
euch . . . . mein Bo - - te, mein Bo - - - te sein.

1st. Tempo. 1o.

To happy
Ich will euch

tr

tr

tr

2nd.
Tempo 1o.
How glad - ly would I there re - pair, And with her all life's bless - ings share, There
Am lieb - sten flog' ich sel - ber hin, Und sagt' ihr wie so treu ich bin, Und
p
pass the hap - py hours a - way, And dream of joys that ne'er de - cay; All care for -
klagt ihr mei - ne lan - ge Pein, dass fern von ihr ich jetzt muss sein; Da läg' ich
Cres e string.
- got, there we would dwell, Lips breathing love, our bliss to tell....... Come
auch, an ih - rer Brust, und Kuss um Kuss. und Lie - bes - lust....... O
Andante Con Molto Espress.
pret - - - ty birds, so glad...... and free, Oh let.... me still more
bitt' euch, lie - - - - be Vö - - - - ge - lein, O bitt'..... euch, lie - - - be
f
Legato.

hap - - - - - py be,   and bear   my vows..... sin -
Vö - - - - - ge - lein,   will keins,   will keins...... von

cere,................ ... ..   To   her.... I love, I love   so
euch.................   mein   Bo - - - te   sein, Bo - - - te

dear,   Come pret - ty birds, so glad and free,
sein,   O bitt' euch lie - be Vö - ge - lein,

Oh let me still more hap - - - py be.
O bitt' euch, lei - be Vö - - - ge - lein.

BRIGHTEST EYES.
(DIE SCHÖNSTEN AUGEN.)

Composed and sung by Stigelli

Andantino appassionato.

Thou'st pearls and dia - monds, fair one, Hast all that men a -
Du hast Dia - man - ten und Per - len, Hast Al - les was Menschen be -
beau - teous eyes of thine, love, I've sung them o'er and
dei - ne schö - nen Au - gen, Hab ich ein gan - zes

Dolce e stringendo.

- dore, And hast the bright - est eyes, love, My dear - est what would'st thou have
gehr, Und hast die schön - sten Au - gen, Mein Lieb - - chen was willst Du noch
o'er, In count - less songs im - mor - tal, My dear - est, what would'st thou have
Heer Von e - - wigen Lie - dern gedich - tet, Mein Lieb - - chen was willst Du noch

p e stringendo.

dolce.
f
1st time.

more! And hast the brightest eyes, love, My dear - est what would'st thou have more? Those
mehr? Und hast die schön - sten Au - gen, Mein Lieb - chen, was willst Du noch mehr? Auf
more? In count - less songs im-mor-tal, My dear - est what would'st thou have
mehr? Von e - wigen Lie-dern gedich-tet, Mein Lieb - chen, was willst Du noch

2'cnd time omit.
rit.

more?   With thy   bright eyes   thou'st pain'd   me,   Man
mehr?   *Mit Dei - - - nen schö - - - nen Au - gen   Hast*

ne'er . . . . was so tortured be - fore.   Down, down   to despair   thou hast
Du . . . . mich ge - quä - let so   sehr,   Und   hast   mich zu Grun - de ge -

brought me,   My   dear - est, what would'st   thou have   more?   With
- rich - tet,   Mein Lieb - - chen, was willst   Du   noch   mehr?   Mit

thy   bright eyes   thou'st pain'd   me,   Man ne'er   was so tor - tur'd be -
Dei - - - nen schö - - - nen Au - gen,   Hast Du   mich ge - quä - let so

fore, Down, down to despair thou hast brought me, My
sehr, Und hast mich zu Grun - de ge rich · · · · tet, Mein

dear - est what would'st thou have more? Down, down to des - pair thou hast
Lieb - - chen was willst Du noch mehr? Und hast mich zu Grun - de ge -

brought me, My dear - - - est what would'st thou have more?
· · · rich · · · tet, Mein Lieb - - - chen, was willst Du noch mehr?

(LAUE LÜFTE, BLUMENDÜFTE.)

Schubert.

Moderato.

1. Flow'rets bloom-ing, Winds per-fum-ing, Ev'-ry joy of youth and spring, Soft ca-
1. Lau - e Lüf - te, Blu - men - düf - te, al - le Lenz und Ju - gend - - lust, fri - scher
2. When the stream-ing Eyes are beam-ing, Thro' the mist of sor - row's tear, There's a
2. Wenn die feuch - ten Au - gen feuch - ten, von der Weh - muth lin - - dem Thau, Dann ent -

ress - es Beauty press - es On the lips that fond-ly cling; Wine cups flow - ing, Nec-tar glow-ing, Mer - ry
Lip - pen Küs - se nip - pen, Sanft ge - wiegt an zar - ter Brust; dann der Trau - ben Nek - tar rau - ben, lži - hen
heal - ing Pow'r re - veal - ing Heav'nly glimpses bright and clear; Oh how fleet - ly, Calm'd thus sweet-ly, Each wild
sie - gelt, D'rinn ye - spie - gelt, Sich dem Blick die Him - mels - au. Wie er - quick - lich Au - gen - blick - lich löscht es

dance and frol - ic arts, All the pas - sions' Wildest fashions, Can they ev - er fill our hearts? Can they
Tanz und Spiel und Scherz, was die Sin - nen nur ge - win - nen, ach, er - füllt es je das Herz? ach, er -
thought to rest is hushed, As the flow - ers, Cool'd by showers, Lift their heads, that erst were cru-h'd, Lift their
je - de uil - de Gluth: Wie vom Re - gen Blu - men pfle-gen he - bet sich der mat - te Muth, he - bet

fp

ev - er fill our hearts?
- füllt es je das Herz?
heads that erst were crush'd.
sich der mat - te Muth.

8va

pp

THE STAR OF HOME.
(DER HEIMATHSTERN.)

Canthal.

Poco Andante.

1. Far from home and all its pleas - ures, Here I
1. Von der Hei -- math weit und fer - ne, Steh' ich
2. None but those who have been part - ed, Know the
2. Nur wer Tren - nung je em - pfun - den, Und die

stand for-lorn, a - lone; Where are ye, my heart's fond treas - ures? List ye not my plaintive moan? Brightly
nun ver-las-sen hier, Se - he wohl die-sel-ben Ster - ne, Doch der Ei - ne feh-let mir. Die - ser
pow'r of mighty love, When for - sa - ken, broken - heart - ed, All our hopes are throned a - bove. Sad re-
wah - re Lieb' ge - fühlt, Kennt den Schmerz von sol - chen Wun - den, Wo-raus im - mer Sehn-sucht quillt. Könnt' ich

gleams the star of ev - en, And my soul it fills with pain, For on yon - der moonlit
Ei - ne nur von Al - len Sist am theu - rr - sten mir war, Denn es wirk - ten sei - ne
- gret, and rest-less long - ing, Day and night my bo-som fill, Dreary thoughts and fancies
ein - mal ihn noch schau - en, Li - ben mich an sei - nem Strahl, Lie - be, Hoff - nung und Ver-

heav - en I would gaze at home a - gain.
Strahlen Auf mich mild und wun-der - bar.
thronging, Are the ex - ile's portion still.
trau - en, Wü - ren dann nur mei - ne Wahl.

IF ON THE MEADS.

(SEH' ICH DIE WEITE GRÜNE AU.)

F. Gumbert.

Allegro Moderato.

1. If on the meads I cast my view,...... Or look on heaven's gladsome blue; If whispers near some ev'ning
1. Seh' ich die wei - te grü - ne Au',...... blick' in des Himmels schönes Blau, lis - pelt ein Ze - phir a-bend
2. If on thine eye I fix my gaze,...... And thou elude my searching rays, If gently thou my hand dost
2. Seh' ich in's lie - be Au - ge dir,...... birgst du das Dei - ne dann vor mir, drückst mir so leis' und warm die

Poco rit. **A Tempo.**

breeze,........ That wakes the rust - ling of the trees,.... If mer - ry birds their voices raise,....
-lich,........ rau - schen die Bäu - me her - um mich,.... sin - - get der Vo - gel munt're Schaar,....
press,........ While not a word thy lips ex - press,.... O then what hap - pi - ness I feel,......
Hand,........ weil ach, dein Mund kein Wört-chen find,.... O viel zu gross ist dann mein Glück,.....

Poco rit. **A Tempo.**

Poco rit. **Cres.** **Mosso. Con molto espress.**

'Tis then my heart so tru - ly says: That I.... do love thee, That I.... do
dann wird es mir im Herzen klar: Dass ich,..... dich lie - - be, dass ich... dich
While all my raptur'd looks reveal: That I..... do love thee, That I.... do
dann sagt' es dir mein heis-ser Blick: Dass ich,..... dich lie - - be, dass ich.... dich

Colla voce. **Rit.** **Mosso Cres.**

_ff_ a piacere. _tr_

love thee, That I do love........... thee......
lie - - be, dass ich dich lie............ be......

_ff_ _p_ Tempo 1.

SERENADE TO IDA.

(STÄNDCHEN AN IDA.)

Weingand.

1. Night a - round ... is soft - ly creep - ing, All the earth to rest is laid; Grief it -
1. Al - les ruht. ..... Wie ab - ge - schie - - den, ab - ge - löst ist je - des Joch; selbst der
2. Tho' a - round ..... these clois - ters night - ly, Spir - its awe the tim - id breast, Love fears
2. Um die na - - he Kirch - hof mau - - er, Wand - eln, wie die Sa - ge spricht, Nächtlich.

- self .... lies calm - ly sleep - ing, Sleepest thou, ... be - lov - ed maid? I - da
Gram .... ents - chlief im Frie - - den, mei - ne Lie - - be, wachst du noch? Hö - re
not, ... where slumb'ring light - ly, I - da lies .... in heav'nly rest, Play - ful
düs - tre Geis - ter - schau - er ; Doch die Lie - - be fürch - tet nicht ! Auch be -

hear .... my lute's soft num - bers, Float - ing on ... the balm - y air. ..... Yet my
mei - - nen letz - ten Laut, Der sich nur der Nacht ver - traut, ... Stö - re
zeph - yrs gent - ly steal - ing, Up - ward waft .... my song to thee, ... May it's
- seelt der Raum mit Muth, Wo die sanf - - te Un - schuld ruht ...... Stö - re, &c.

lute, ... if I - da slum - bers, Hush! nor wake .... my la - dy fair ......
du ...... mein Lau - ten ton. ...... I - da nicht, sie schlummert schon ....
tones .... my love re - veal - ing, Fill thy dreams .. with thoughts of me. ......

O WERT THOU BUT MINE OWN, LOVE.
(O WENN DU WÄRST MEIN EIGEN.)

Kücken.

1. O, wert thou but mine own, love, How
1. Ach wenn du wärst mein ei - gen, wie
2. O, wert thou but mine own, love, How
2. Ach wenn du wärst mein ei - gen, wie

dear thou'dst be to me! Deep, deep with - in my heart, love, I'd cher - ish on - ly thee! My
lieb sollt'st Du mir sein! wie wollt' ich tief im Her - zen nur he - gen Dich al - lein, und
bright this world would be! I'd have no more to wish, love, But still to gaze on thee. I'd
wär die Welt dann schön, es blie - be nicht zu wün - schen; als Dich stets an zu sehn; und

ev' - ry trea - sure, ev' - ry joy I'd seek in thy love beam-ing eye. O wert thou but mine own, love. How
al - le Wonn' und al - les Glück mir schö - pfen nur aus Dei - nem Blick; Ach wenn Du wärst mein ei - gen, wie
prize nought else of earth - ly joy, If met by thy love beaming eye, O wert thou, &c.
ganz ver - sun - ken in mein Glück er - hielt die Welt nicht ei - nen Blick; Ach wenn du, &c.

dear, how dear thou'dst be. How dear,...... how dear........ to me.
lieb sollt'st Du mir sein, wie lieb,..... wie lieb sollt'st Du mir sein.

LOVE'S REQUEST.

(LIEBES BITTE.)

A. Reichardt.

Cantabile. Con Espress.

1. Now the day is slowly waning; Evening breezes soft-ly, soft-ly moan. Wilt thou ne'er heed my com-
1. *Wie die Blüm - lein draussen flat-tern, In der A - bend-lüf - - - te weh'n.* Und du willst mir's Herz ver-
2. Can'st thou thus unmov'd behold me, Still untouch'd by love, by love so deep? Nay, thine arms more closely
2. *Hab' ge - liebt dich oh - ne En - de Hab' dir nie ein Leid . . , ... ge - than.* Und du drückst mir still die

- plaining? Can'st thou leave me thus a - lone? Stay with me, ... my dar - ling, stay, . . . And like a
- *bit - tern, Und du willst schon wie - der geh'n!* *Bleib bei mir . . . . . und geh' nicht fort.* *In mei - nem*
- fold me, And thine eyes be - gin to weep. Stay with me, ... my dar - ling, stay, . . . And like a
- *Hän - de, Und du fängst zu wei - nen an.* *Wei - ne nicht . . . . und geh' nicht fort.* *In mei - nem*

Un poco ritard. **Un poco piu Cres.** **Cres -- cen -- do.**

dream thy life shall pass a - way. Stay with me, ... my darling, stay, And like a dream thy life shall pass a-
Her - zen ist der schön - ste Ort. *Bleib bei mir, ... und geh' nicht fort.* *In mei - nem Herzen ist der schönste*
dream thy life shall pass a - way. Stay with me, ... my darling, stay, And like a dream thy life shall pass a-
Wei - ne nicht . . . . . . und geh' nicht fort. *In mei - nem Herzen ist der schönste*

Ritard colla voce. **Un poco piu Cres.** **Cres -- cen -- do.**

- way, . . like a dream shall pass a - way.
- *Ort . . . . der schönste, der schön - ste Ort.*

Poco animato.

No ro - gret ... shall e'er at - tend thee, Ne'er shall sor - row dim thine eye, 'Gainst the
Oh da drau - - ssen, in der Fer - ne, Sind die Men - schen nicht so gut, Und ich

Ritard.

Cre - - scen - - - do. **Ritard.**

world's alarms to fend ... thee, Glad - ly. proudly .... will I die .... Stay with
gäb' für dich so ger - - - ne, Mein Le - - ben und mein Blut. ...... Bleib bei

pp

pp **Molto Ritard.**

me, then, darling. stay, And like a dream, thy life shall pass a - way, Stay with me, my darling,
mir, und geh' nicht fort, In mei - nem Her - zen ist der schön - ste Ort, Bleib bei mir, und geh' nicht

pp **Tremolo.**

stay, And like a dream thy life shall pass a - way, shall pass .... a - way ....
fort, In mei - nem Her - zen ist der schönste Ort, der schön - ste Ort. ....

Cres. Molto. *f* *f* **Cres.** *f* *f*

THE YOUNG RECRUIT.

Written and Arranged by GEORGE LINLEY.

Composed by KUCKEN.

Allegretto.

1. See ! these rib - bons gai - ly stream - - - ing, I'm a sol - - dier now, Li - zette, I'm a sol - dier now, Li - zette; Yes, of bat - - tle I am dream - - - ing, And the hon - - or I .... shall get................ With a sa - bre by my
2. We will march a - - - way, to - - - mor - - - row, At the break - ing of the day, At the break - ing of the day ; And the Lrum - pets will be sound - - - ing, And the mer - - ry cym - bals play............. Yet be - fore I say good
3. Shame ! Li - zette, to still be weep - - - ing, While there's fame in store for me, While there's fame in store for me ; Think when Lome I am re - - turn - - - ing, What a joy - - ful day 'twill be,.............. When to church you're fond - ly

mf Ped. Cres. *mf* Cres. Bea marcato. *p* *pp* Dolce.

side, And a hel-met on my brow, And a proud steed to ride, I shall
bye, And a last sad part-ing take, As a proof of your love, Wear this
led, Like some La-dy smart-ly drest, And a he-ro you shall wed, With a

rush on the foe: Yes, I flat-ter me, Li-zette, 'Tis a
gift for my sake: Then, cheer up, my own Li-zette, Let not
med-al on his breast: Ha! there's not a maid-en fair, But with

life that well will suit, The gay life of a young Re---
grief your beau-ty stain, Soon you'll see the Re-cruit a---
wel-come will sa-lute, The gay bride of the young Re---

cruit,............ The gay life of a young Re--cruit.
gain.......... .... Soon you'll see the Re-cruit a--gain.
cruit,........ .... The gay bride of the young Re--cruit

FLY, MY SKIFF, AMID THE ROSES.

(DIE ERWARTUNG.)

F. Kücken.

Agitato.

1. Fly, my
1. Flie - ge,
2. Balmy
2. Würz'- ge

skiff, a - mid the ro - - ses, Fly, the smil - - - ing shore to greet! In that
Schiff - lein, durch die Ro - - sen des Ge - - sta - - des her vom See! Hier darf
breez - es, gent - ly blow - - ing, Bring my soul's.... a - dored to me! Mur - mur
Lüf - te kommt ge - flo - - gen, Bringst schnell... mein Liebchen mir! Mur - melt

grove my love re - po - - ses, There what joy.... a - gain to meet! Anx - ious
ich mit Lirtchen ko - - sen, wie ist mir.... so wohl, so wohl! Ach! wie
loud - - er, wa - ters flow - - ing, Tell her of........ my con - stan - cy! Peace and
lau - - ter kla - re Wo - - gen, sagt von mei - - ner Lie - be ihr! Wie - der

thoughts my bo - som thrill, Oh de - lay........ not, dear - est, still! Anxious
schlägt das Herz so bang'! zau - dre, Hol - - de, nicht zu lang', ach! mein
joy........ my heart be - guile, Does my loved.... one but smile! Peace and
keh - - ren Freud' und Ruh, lä - - chelt Lieb - - chen mir nur zu, wie - der

First system:

thoughts my bo-som thrill, ... Oh de - lay not, dear - est, still, Anx - ious
Herz, es schlägt so bang'! .... zau - dre, Hol - de, nicht so lang', och! wie
joy .... my heart be - guile, ... Does my loved one ... but smile. Peace and
keh - ren Freud und Ruh, ... lä - chelt Lieb - chen mir ..... nur zu, wie - der

sf pdim. p Dim.

Second system:

thoughts my bo - som thrill, Oh de - lay ...... not, dear-est, still! Anxious
schlägt das Herz so bang'! zau - dre, Hol - de, nicht so lang'! ach! wie
joy ...... my heart be - guile, Does my loved ... one but smile! Peace and
keh - ren Freud'und Ruh, lä - chelt Lieb - chen mir nur zu, wie - der

Third system:

thoughts my bo - som thrill, ... Oh de - lay not, dear - est, still! Oh de -
schlägt das Herz so bang'! zau - dre, Hol - de, nicht so lang', zau - dre,
joy my heart be - guile, ... Does my loved one but smile. Does my
keh - ren Freud' und Ruh, lä - chelt Lieb - chen mir nur zu, lä - chelt

dim. dol.
molto cres. f dim. dol.

Fourth system:

- lay .... not, dear - est, still! Oh de - lay ...... not, still!
Hol - de, nicht zu lang'! zau - dre, Hol - de, nicht lang'!
loved .... one but smile! Does my loved ...... one but smile.
Lieb - chen mir nur zu, lä - chelt Lieb - chen mir zu!

ritard.
ritard.

IMPATIENCE.

(UNGEDULD.)

Fr. Curschmann.

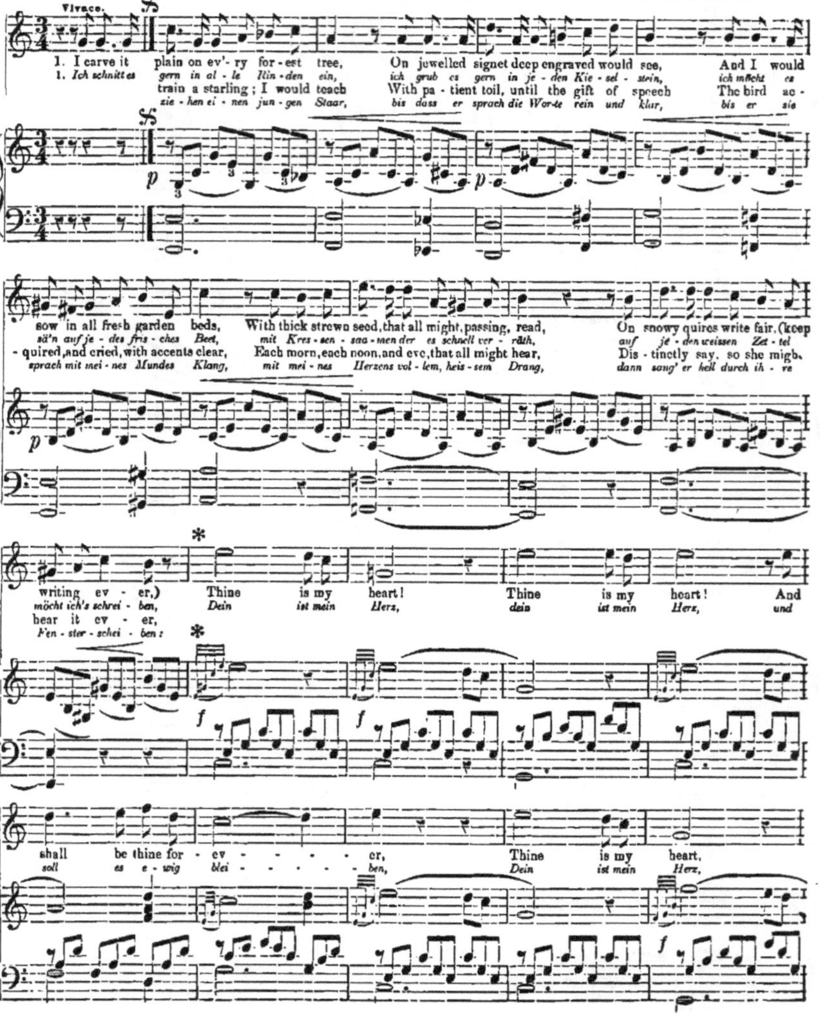

Thine   is my heart! And shall be thine   for - - ev - - - - er.
dein   ist mein Herz! und soll es e - - - - wig blei - - ben.

2nd Verse D. C. to the Sign. 𝄋

3d & 4th Verse continue to end of page, then to the Sign. ✻

2. And I   would
2. *Ich möcht' mir*
3. On morn - ing
3. *Den Mor - gen -*
4. It must be
4. *Ich mein, es*

Fine.

winds the fond word comes to me, On pear - ly rain drops e'er reflect - ed see, On flow'r leaves painted, and on insect
win - den macht' ich hauchen ein, ich möcht es sau - sein durch den re - gen Hain.
printed on my longing eyes. It blush - es on my cheek in rud - dy dyes, And you may read it on my lips tho'
müsst in mei - nen Au - gen stehn, auf mein - en Wangen müsst man's brennen sehn, zu le - sen wärs auf meinen stummen

wings, I hear it when each happy warbler sings, And waves to frame the sentence dear en-deav - or,
- stern. Trug es der Duft zu ihr von nah und fern. Ihr Wogen, könt ihr nicht als Rä - der trei - ben:
still, And ev' - ry breath repeat, without my will,— But she of all hears not, nor see-eth ev - er,—
Mund, ein je - der A - themzug gab's laut ihr kund, und sie merkt nichts von all' dem ban - gem Trei - ben.

D. S. ✻ al Fine.

THE SCARLET SARAFAN.

(DER ROTHE SARAFAN.)

Russian Air.

Mother, don't at-tempt to sew the scar-let sa-ra-fan, For thy ef-fort would be use-less,
Nä - he, Mut-ter, nä - he nicht den ro - then Sa - ra - fin, Dei - ne Mü - he ist ver - lor - en,

and thy la-bour vain. Daughter, cease thy fol - ly, and do not talk so fast, Know that youth's gay
quälet dich nur dar - an. Töch - ter - lein dein Köpf - chen ist noch nicht recht ge - scheid, Wis - se nur, nicht

morn-ing, Will not always last. Though thou art so mer - ry, and so much at ease,
e - wig währt die Ju - gend - zeit. Springst du auch so lu - stig, und singst im grü - nen Wald,

Song will fail to cheer thee, and the dance to please. When at length the ro - ses
Tanzlust, ach, ver - ge - het und Ge - sang ver - hallt. Blei - chen erst die Wan - gen

* SARAFAN.—The dress of Russian young women.

from thy cheeks do flee, Youth with all its plea - sures, seems but va - ni - ty,
dir in ern - ster Zeit, Fühlst du dass die Ju - gend nichts als Ei - tel - keit,

Youth with all its plea - sures, seems but va - ni - ty. Do not smile, but give an ear to
Fühlst du dass die Ju - gend nichts als Ei - tel - keit. Lache nicht, und glau - be nur was

what thy moth-er says; Rap-id - ly youth's bloom is past, and beauty soon de - cays. Yet when thee I
dei - ne Mutter sagt; Schnell vergeht der Ju - gend Spur. Dem Himmel sei's ge - klagt. Doch wenn ich dich

see and look on, I am young a - gain; Sing and dance, but with thy trifling, cause me no more pain.
seh' und hö - re, Werd ich wie - der jung— Sing und spring, doch nim - mer stö - re mir Er - in - ner - ung.

HOME! MY OWN DEAR MOUNTAIN HOME!
(DIE HEIMATH.)

C. Krebs.

Allegretto.

1. Home! my own dear mountain home, Joy-ous-ly to thee I come!
1. In der Hei - math ist es schön, auf der Ber - ge lich - ten Höh'n,
2. Round my mountain home the breeze Wakes sweet music in the trees;
2. In der Hei - math ist es schön, wo die Lüf - te sanf - ter weh'n,

Ev' - ry rug - ged peak, whose snows With the drooping clouds are blending; Ev' - ry field with
auf der Ber - ge lich - ten Höh'n, auf den schroffen Fel - sen Pfa - den, auf der Flu - ren
There, from many a rook - y well, Wa - ters bright are ev - er springing, With their sil - ver
wo die Lüf - te sanf - ter weh'n, wo des Ba - ches Sil - ber - wei - sse murmelnd eilt von

harvest bend - ing; Ev' - ry tree, its shade ex - tend - ing, Where the gen - tle
grünen Saa - ten; auf der Flu - ren grünen Saa - ten; wo die Heer - den
rip - ples sing - ing! There too, happier voi - ces ring - ing, Where belov - ed
Stell'zu Stel - le; murmelnd eilt von Stell'zu Stel - le; wo der El - tern

berds re - pose, Tell of thee, dear mountain home! Joy - ous - ly to thee I come,
weid - end gehn, in der Hei - math ist es schön, wo die Heer - den wei - dend gehn,
kindred dwell, Tell of thee, dear mountain home! Joy - ous - ly to thee I come,
Häu - ser stehn, in der Hei - math ist es schön, wo der El - tern Häu - ser stehn,

Home, my own dear mountain home! Home!.... my own dear moun - - tain home! la - - - i la -
in der Hei - math ist es schön, in .... der Hei - math ist es schön! la - - i la

- - - - i la la la la la - - - i la la la - - - i la la -

- - - i la la la la la la.

THE SONG OF SPRING.

(FRÜHLING'S-LIED.)

Mendelssohn.

The spring in wrath com-men-ces, With storm-y wind and rain, He
Der Früh-ling naht mit Brau-sen, er rü-stet sich zur That,

For-get thy win-ter sor-row, With joy receive thy guest, He
Thu' ab die Win-ter sor-gen: em-pfan-ge frisch den Gast; er

breaks thro' winter's fen-ces, And green comes o'er the plain, He breaks thro' winter's
un-ter Sturm und Sau-sen krimt still die grü-ne Saat; und un-ter Sturm und

flies like dawning mor-row, Nor stays he long to rest, He flies like dawning
fliegt wie jun-ger Mor-gen; er hält nicht lan-ge Rast; er fliegt wie jun-ger

fen-ces, And green, and green comes o'er the plain, Then wake, O man, thy vi-gils
Sau-sen keimt still, keimt still die grü-ne Saat; drum wach, er-wach', du Men-schen-

mor-row, Nor stays he long, not long to rest. The bud it swells, the flower
Mor-gen; er hält nicht lan-ge, nicht lange Rast. Die Knospe schwellt, die Blu-me

keep,.... And let not spring find thee a - sleep.   Then wake, O man..........
kind,.... dass dich der Lenz nicht schlafen! find'!   Drum wach', er - wach',

blows,... The moments haste, and spring-time flows,   O there - fore wake........
blüht,.... die Stunde eilt, der Frühling flieht.

thy vi - gils keep.......   And let not spring find thee a -
du Men - schen-kind.......   dass dich der Lenz nicht schla....fend

- - sleep,   And let not spring find thee..........
find'!   dass dich der Lenz nicht schla - - - fend

sleep.
find')

poco più lento.

Cast, Son of earth, be-bind thee The bonds which round thee cling, Break, break the chains that bind' thee, And
Dir ar - men Menschen - kin - de ist wund und weh ums Herz? auf, spreng' ge - trost die Rin - - e, schau

look towards the spring. The ice will melt.... the streams will flow........ Thy troubles
mu - thig Frühling - wärts! Es schmilzt das Eis...... die Quel - le rinnt......... dir thut der

o'er, thy joys will grow, Then as the lark up - ris - ing, Pours forth his joy a - loud. Let
Schmerz und löst' sich lind. Und wie die Vög - lein lei - - se an - stim - men ih - ren Chor, so -

be thy heart's re-joic - ing. A - mong the mirth-ful crowd. Thou art not lone, art not be-
schall' auch dei - ne Wei - se aus tief - ster Brust her - vor..... Bist nicht ver - armt, bist nicht al

reft, . . . While yet there's song and sun - shine left. Thou art not lone, ...
lein, umringt von Sang und Son - nen schein! Bist nicht ver - armt, ...
Sf
Cres.
pp
Cres - cen - do.
f
art not be - reft, ... While yet there's song and sun - shine
bist nicht al - lein, ... um - ringt von Sang und Son - - - nen - -
dim.
p
left, While yet there's song and sun - - - - shine
schein' um - - - ringt von Sang und Son - - - - - - nen -
left, there's song and sun - - - - - - - - - shine left.
schein, von Sang und Son - - - - - - - - - - nen - schein.
Sf
rit.
Ped.

THE TEAR

(DIE THRÄNE.)

F. Gumbert.

Andante.

1. With trembling step, in life we scarce ap - pear, Ere on the cheek is seen the glist'ning tear; First glad - ly
1. *Macht man in's Le - ben kaum den er - sten Schritt, bringt man als Kind schon ei - ne Thrä - ne mit, und Freu - den -*
2. How beauteous shines the fond tear of the bride, When he she loves is kneeling by her side; Their hearts are
2. *Wie schön ist doch die Thrä - ne ei - ner Braut, wenn dem Ge - lieb - ten sie in's Au - ge schaut, man schlingt das*

springs the welcome tear of bliss, When child and mother share the tender kiss. As years advance,'mid chequer'd joys and
thrä - nen giebt als er - sten Gruss, dem Kind die Mut - ter mit dem er - sten Kuss; man wächst em - por dann zwischen Freud' und
one, the vow of truth is taken: To share till death each other's care and pain; If o'er his soul, hope lose its soothing
Band, sie wer - den Weib und Mann, da geht der Kampf mit Noth und Sor - gen an.

woes, The heart ex - pands, like some sweet op' - ning rose; The gen - tle girl, to him she holds most
Schmerz, da zieht die Lie - be in das jun - ge Herz, und of - fen - bart das Herz der Jung - frau
pow'r, The faith - ful wife can cheer the lone - some hour; Con - fid - ing still, she points to worlds more
lor, blickt noch das Weib ver - trau - ungs - voll em - por, zur Ster - nen - welt, zum hei - tren Him - mels -

dear, Her love be - trays with one soft tim - id tear, Her love be - trays with one soft tim - id tear.
sich, spricht ei - ne Thrä - ne: ja ich lie - be dich, spricht ei - ne Thrä - ne: ja ich lie - be dich.
fair, And with a tear, says kindly, "don't despair!" And with a tear, says kindly, "don't despair!"
licht, und ei - ne Thrä - ne spricht: ver - za - ge nicht, ja ei - ne Thrä - ne spricht: ver - za - ge nicht.

SHE IS MINE.

(BÄCHLEIN, LASS DEIN RAUSCHEN SEIN.)

F. Curschmann.

Cease thy murmurs, tinkling rill;
Bächlein, lass dein Rauschen sein,

Thou too, bu-sy wheel, be still; Hush your
Rä - der, stellt eu'r Brau-sen ein, All ihr

strains, sweet birds on hedge and spray; No song but
mun - - - tern Wald - vö - ge - lein, gross und klein, endet, en - - det

mine must wake to - day; Yet I call up - on all, Come, with
eu - - re Me - lo - dein durch den Hain, aus und ein schal - le

me their voic - es join,   in   cho - - - - rus join,   "She   is   mine,   the
heut' ein Reim al - lein,   *ein*   *Reim   al - lein,*   *"Die   ge - - lieb - - - - te*

mill - er's love - ly   maid,   She   is   mine!   She   is   mine,   The   mill - er's love - ly
Müll - er - in ist   mein,   *ist   mein!*   *die   ge -   lieb - - - - te   Müll - er - in ist*

maid!   is   mine!   she's   mine! . . . .   she's   mine!"
mein,   *ist   mein,*   *ist   mein,. . . . .   ist   mein!"*

1st. time.

Spring! hast thou no   fair - er flow'rs than   these to show?
Früh - ling sind das   al - le dei - ne   Blüme - - lein.

Sun! hast thou no beams that bright er glow? Say, oh must I all a-
Son - ne, hast du kei - - - nen an - dern Schein? O so muss ich ganz al -

- lone make my heart's glad full - ness known? Oh! 'tis so fraught with hap - pi - ness, it
- lein mit dem sel' - gen Wor - te mein, un - ver - - stan - den in der

must, it will o'er - flow! It must, it will o'er - flow! . . . .
wei - - ten, wei - - - ten Schö - - pfung sein . . . .

Ritard.   2nd. time.
. . . . . it will o'er - flow! . . . . mine!
. . . . mein?

AH! COULD I TEACH THE NIGHTINGALE.

Keller.

1. Ah! could I teach the Night-in-gale, Three lit-tle words to num-ber, Then

2. How oft I've sought the Night-in-gale, By spring and sha-dy bow-er,

should its sweet voice from the vale Break on thy morning slum-ber, Then

That to my soul her plaintive tale, Might speak with mu-sic's pow-er, That

should its sweet voice from the vale, Break on thy morn-ing slum-ber; Ere

to my soul her plaintive tale, Might speak with mu-sic's pow-er, Yet morn - ing's dawn there should she be,   Be - fore   thy win - dow greet - ing,   In

oh! be - lieve me ne'er could be,   So wel - come her sweet greet - ing,

mf

soft - est tones re - peat-ing: I love thee, I love thee well,   For - get,   for-get me

In softest tones re - peat-ing,   I love thee, I love thee well,   For - get,   forget me

p   pp

not,   I love,   I love thee   well,   Oh! then for-get me not.

not,   I love, I love thee   well,   Oh! then for - get me not.

ALL IS OVER.

Weber.

All is o - ver, we are parted, Lost the light of life's young day ; Now forlorn and broken-

hearted, Must I take my weary way. Love - ly girl, I think with sad - ness On the day that first we

met, Then a - rose my sun of gladness, Ah ! how soon, how soon that sun has set. Oh ! what

bliss - ful joy, what plea - sure Round my youth - ful heart I wove, Then my songs were gay and joy-ous, For the theme of all was love, For the

theme of all was love, Now I wan-der forth de-ject-ed, Nothing

car-ing where I go, And my songs are all neg-lect-ed, Save some

mourn-ful strain of woe, Save some mourn-ful strain of woe.

THE ERL · KING.

(WER REITET SO SPÄT.)

Schubert.

Who rid - - eth so late through the
Wer rei - - tet so spät durch

night - wind wild? It is the fa - - ther with his
Nacht und Wind? Es ist der Va - ter mit sei - - - nem

child;   He has   the   lit - tle   one   well   in his   arm,   He holds   him
Kind: Er hat   den   Kna - - ben   wohl   in   den   Arm,   Er fasst ihn

safe, and he folds   him   warm.   My
sich - er, er   hält   ihn   warm.   Mein

son,   why hid - est thy face   so   shy?   Seest   thou not,
Sohn,   was birgst du so bang   dein Ges - icht?   Siehst, Va - - - ter,

fa - - - ther, the Erl - - - King   nigh?   The Er - - - len -
du . . . . den Erl - - - Kö - nig nicht?   Den Er - - - - len -

King with train and crown?   It is a
Kö - nig mit Kron' und Schweif?   _Mein Sohn, es_

wreath of mist, my son.   Come, love . . . . . ly
ist ein Ne - bel-streif.   _Du lie . . . . . bes_

boy, come, go with me;   Such mer . . . . ry
Kind, komm, geh mit mir!   _Gar Schö . . . . ne_

plays I will play . . . . with thee.   Ma . . . . ny a
Spie . . . le spiel . . . . ich mit dir; Manch' bun . . . . . te

bright flow - er grows on the strand, And my moth - er has ma - ny a gay
Blu - - men sind an - - dem Strand; Meine Mut - ter hat manch

gar - - - - - ment at hand. My fa - ther, my fa - ther, and dost thou not
gül - - - - - den Ge - wand. Mein Va - ter, mein Va - ter, und hö - rest du

hear what the Erl - King whispers in my ear? Be qui - et, ah! be
nicht, was Er - len - König mir lei - - se ver - spricht? Sei ru - hig, bleibe

still, my child; through withered leaves the wind howls wild. Come,
ru - hig, mein Kind; in dür - ren Blät - tern säu - selt der Wind. Willst

56   THE ERL - KING, Continued

love - ly boy, wilt thou go with me? My daugh-ters fair shall wait on thee, My
fei - - ner Kna - be du mit mir gehn? Meine Tüch - ter sol - len dich war - ten schön, Mann

daugh - ters their night - ly rev - els keep. They'll sing and they'll dance, and they'll rock thee to sleep, They'll
Töch - ter füh - - ren den nächt - lichen Reihn, Und wie - gen und tan - zen und sin - gen dich ein, Sie

sing, and they'll dance, and they'll rock thee to sleep. My fa - - ther, my fa - - ther, and
wie - gen und tan - - zen und sin - gen dich ein. Mein Va - - ter, mein Va - ter, und

seest thou not The Erl - King's daugh-ters in yon dim spot? My
siehst du nicht dort, Erl - Kö - nig's Töch - ter am fin - stern Ort? Mein

son, my son, I see and I know 'Tis the old gray wil-low that
Sohn, mein Sohn, ich seh' es ge-nau. Es schein-en die al-ten

shim - - mers so. I
Wei - - den so grau. Ich

love.... thee, thy beau-ty has ravished my sense; And wil-ling or not, I will
lie - - be dich, mich reizt deine schö-ne Ge-stalt, Und bist du nicht wil-lig, so

car - - ry thee hence. O fa - - ther the Erl-King now puts forth his arm,
brauch ich Ge-walt. Mein Va - - ter, mein Va-ter, jetzt fasst er mich an,

Fa - ther the Erl - King has done me harm.
Erl - Kö - nig hat mir ein Leid ge - than.

fa - - - ther shud-ders, he hur - ries on; And fas - - ter he
Va - - - ter grau-set's, er rei - tet ge - schwind; Er hält in

holds his moan - - - ing son; He reach - es his
Ar - men das äch - - zen-de Kind; Er reicht den

home with fear and dread, Lo! in his arms the child was dead.
Hof mit Müh' und Noth; In sei-nen Ar - men das Kind war todt.

NEAR THEE!
NAH.

Lindblad.

Poco Allegretto.

Birds blithe are sing-ing | In the heavens clear; | In val-leys spring-ing.
Vög - lein in Lüf - ten | *singt so laut und schön,* | *Blüm - lein der Trif - ten*
Youth has de - part - ed. | Soon, a - las, it fled! | Would that, light-heart - ed,
So ist ver - schwunden | *mei - ne Ju - gend schön;* | *ob ich ge - fun - den*

Flow'rs sweet ap - pear; | Song and flow'r de - light not me, | Since I once have gazed on thee,
lüsst sich lie - blich sehn. | *Doch seitdem ich dich er - blickt,* | *nicht mich Sang noch Blü' entzürkt.*
Peace were mine in - stead! | For - mer joys are chang'd to woes, | Grief a - lone my spir - it knows,
Frie - den mir zum Lohn? | *Seuf - zer stei - gen aus der Brust,* | *ach wo blieb die al - te Lust!*

Nought hath gladness, For my mad-ness | Hears and sees but thee! | Song and flow'r de-light me not,
bin voll - kom-men wie be - nom - men, | *hör und seh nur dich!* | *doch seit - dem ich dich er - blickt,*
Love's sweet madness, With thy sadness | Leave me to re - pose! | For me joys are chang'd to woes,
Her - zen's - klage süsse Pla - ge | *lass mich doch in Ruh,* | *Seuf - zer steigen aus der Brust,*

Since I once have gazed on thee, | Nought hath gladness, For my mad-ness | Hears and sees but thee!
nicht mich Sang noch Blü' entzürkt. | *bin voll - kom-men wie be - nom - men,* | *hör und seh nur dich!*
Grief a - lone my spi - rit knows, | Love's sweet madness, With thy sad-ness, | Leave me to re - pose.
ach, wo blieb die al - te Lust! | *Her - zens - klage süsse Pla - ge,* | *lass mich doch in Ruh!*

ADELAIDE.

Beethoven.

Lone - ly wan - - ders thy friend in spring's green gar - den, Mild - ly
Ein - sam wan - - delt dein Freund im Früh - lings Gar - ten, mild vom

stream - eth the ma - gic light a - round him, As through trem - - - - bling blos - som twigs it
lieblichen Zau - ber - licht um - flos - sen, das durch wan - - - - - kende Blü - then - zwei - ge

quivers, A - de - la - i - de, A - de - la - i - de.
zit - tert, A - de - la - i - de, A - de - la - i - de.

In the mir - ror-like stream, in snows on Alp-hills, In the
In der spie - gelnden Fluth, im Schnee der Al - pen, in des
van - ish-ing daylight's golden cloudlets, In the fields of the stars, too, gleams thine image, thine
sin - ken-den Ta - ges Goldge - wölke, im Ge - fil - - de der Sterne strahlt dein Bildniss, dein
im - age, A - de-la - i - de! In the vanishing daylight's golden cloudlets. In the
Bild - niss, A - de - la - i - de! In des sin - kenden Tages Gold-ge - wölke, im Ge -
fields of the stars, too, gleams thine image, thine im - age,
- fil - de der Ster - ne strahlt . . . . . dein Bildniss, dein Bild - niss,

A - - - - de-la - i - de,
A - - - - de-la - i - de,

Ev' - ning winds in the ten - der leaves are whisp'ring.
A - - - bend - lüft - chen im zar - ten Lau - be flüstern,

Sil - ver may - bells a - mid the cool grass rustling, Waters murm'ring, and
Sil - ber - glöck - chen des May's im Grase säuseln, Wellen rau - schen, und

night - in - gales keep fluting, Waters murm'ring, and
Nach - ti - gal - len flö - ten, Wel-len rau - schen, und

night - in - gales keep flut - - - - - ing, A - - - de - - la - i - - - - - - -
Nach - ti - gal - len flö - - - - - - - - - ten, A - - - - de - - - la - i - - - - - - - - - -
p
p
pp
- - de! Evening winds in the ten - der leaves are whisp'ring, Silver May - bells a - mid the cool grass
- de! Abend - lüft - chen im zar - ten Lau - be flüstern, Silber - glöck - chen des May's im Gra - se
rustling, Waters murm'ring, and nightingales keep flut - ing, and nightin-gales keep flut - ing:
säuseln, Wellen rauschen, und Nach - ti - gal - len flö - ten und Nach - ti - gal - len flö - ten,
ff
p
A - - - de - - - la - i - de! A - - - de - - - la - i - de!
A - - - de - - - - la - i - de! A - - - - de - - - - la - i - de!
f
V.S.

Allegro molto.

Soon, O won-der! O won-der! up-on my grave be-hold it,
Einst, O Wun-der! O Wun-der! ent-blüht auf mein-em Gra-be

O won-der! up-on my grave be-hold it,
O Wun-der! ent-blüht auf mei-nem Gra-be

Springs a flow-'ret from out my heart's cold ash-es, yes, from out my
ei-ne Blu-me der Asche meines Her-zens, der..... A-sche

heart's cold ash-es; Plain-ly glimmers, plain-ly glimmers on
mei-nes Her-zens; deut-lich schimmert, deut-lich schimmert auf

Cres.

ev'-ry pur-ple pe-tal, on ev'-ry pur-ple pe-tal: A-de-la
je-dem Purpur-blättchen, auf jedem Purpur-blättchen: A-de-la-
fp
fp
p
-i-de! A-de-la-i-de!
-i-de! A-de-la-i-de!
Cres.
f
sf
Soon, O won-der! soon, O wonder!
Einst, O Wun-der! einst, O Wunder!
sf
p
f
sf
p
Yes, soon on my grave, yes on my grave be-hold it,
ent-blüht, ach ent-blüht auf mei-nem Gra-be
f
f
p

Springs a flow - 'ret from out my heart's cold ash - es. Springs a flow'ret from
ei - ne Blume der Asche mei - nes Her - zens, der A - - sche

out my heart's ash - es; Plain - ly glimmers, plain - ly glimmers, on ev'ry purple
mei - nes Her - zens; deut - lich schimmert, deut - lich schimmert auf je - dem Pur - pur-

pe - tal, on ev-'ry pur-ple pe-tal; A - de-la - i - de,
- blättchen, auf je - dem Pur-pur - blättchen: A - de-la - i - de,

A - - - - - - de-la - i - de, Plainly glimmers on
A - - - - - - de-la - i - - - de; deutlich schimmert auf

ev' - ry pur - ple pe - tal, on ev' - ry pur - ple pe - tal:
je - dem Pur-pur blätt - chen, auf je - dem Pur - pur - blätt - chen:

A . . . . . de - la - i . . . . . . de,
A . . . . de la i . . . . de,

A . . . . . de la i . . . . . . de,
A . . . . . de la . . . i . . . . de,

A . . . . de - la - i . . . . . . de.
A . . . . . de . . la i . . de.

Fine.

AMID THIS GREENWOOD SMILING.

(HIER AN DEM GRÜNEN WALDE.)

S. Thalberg.

A - mid this greenwood smil - ing, Once stood a love - ly cot, A hunts-man's blooming
Hier on dem grü - nen Wal - de, Stand einst ein net - tes Haus, Da ging des Jä - gers

daugh - ter Shed beau - ty o'er the spot. And when a - broad she wan - der'd, Then
Toch - ter, Die schö - ne, ein und aus. Und wenn sie kam ge - gan - gen, War

I was ev - er nigh; When friend - ly I ad - dress'd her, So sweet was her re - ply!
ich ge - wiss nicht fern; Ich grüss - te sie so freun - dlich, Mir dank - te sie so gern!

The huntsman hath de - part - ed, The maiden too, is
Der Jä - ger ist ge - zo - gen, Aus die - ser Gegend

gone,   The cot in ru - ins fall - ing,   Is des - o - late and lone;   A wil - low shall be
fort   Das Haus ward ab - ge - bro - chen.   Und still ist nun der Ort;   Ein Bäum - lein will ich

plant - ed   Up - on   this orphan ground.   Oh, tree! may'st thou still flour - - ish, And
pflan - zen   auf den   verwais - ten Grund.   Du Bäum - lein, blü - he kräf - - tig, Und

bloom   all fresh and sound!   When age at length comes o'er me,   I'll
blei - - be mir ge - sund!   Ich will in dei - nem Schat - ten,   Als

seek this sha - dy spot,   To dream of that fair maid - en,   And of the huntsman's cot.
Greis noch ruh - en aus,   Und von dem Jä - ger träu - men,   Und von des Jä - ger's Haus.

EVENING.
(GUTE NACHT.)

Franz Abt.

Rather slow.

f   *pp*   Legato.

1. In the west the sun de - clin - ing, Sinks be - neath the
1. Son - ne nei - get sich und sin - ket hin - ter Ber - ges-
2. In the wind the grass is bend - ing, Flow'rs now slum - ber
2. Hälm - lein in dem Win - de schwan - ken, Blüm - lein nick - en

Cres.

mountain height,   Tints the clouds with gold - en lin - ing, Sets the hills with ru - bies
höhn zur Ruh,   Rein im Fei - er - glanz sie blin - ket, ihr - er lie - ben Er - de
in the shade;   Birds to seek their nests are wend - ing, Flocks in fold the shep - herds
schlummer - voll,   Bäu - me mit den Ep - feu - ran - ken, Al - le grüs - sen sich und

mf

shin - ing. Then bids all the world good - night!...... Good - night, good -
win - ket still den A - bend - gruss sie zu?.......... Gu - te nacht, gu - te
tend - ing. Home - ward hies the moun - tain maid......... Good - night, good -
dan - ken Freud - er - füllt und kum - mer voll:.......... Gu - te nacht, gu - te

mf   Rall e Dim.

- night!   Good - night, good - night!
nacht,   gu - te Nacht, gu - te Nacht!

Dim.   *p*   *pp*

(DEN LIEBEN LANGEN TAG.)

1. The long, long wea - ry day, Is pass'd in tears a-way, The long, long wea - ry day, Is pass'd in tears away, And
1. Den lie - ben lan - gen Tag Hab i nur Schmertz und Plag, Den lie - ben lan - gen Tag Hab i nur Schmertz und Plag, Und
2. When I, his truth to prove, Would trifle with my love, When I, his truth to prove, would trifle with my love, He'd
2. Er hat mir's oft ge - sagt, Wenn i ihn hab gep-lagt, Er hat mir's oft ge - sagt, Wenn i ihn hab geplagt, Du

still at evening. I am weeping, When from my window's height, I look out on the night, I still am weeping, My lone watch
muss am A - bend doch nur wei - na, Wenn i am Fen - ster steh, und in die Nacht naus seh, Da muss i wei - na, Bin i al -
say, "for me thou shalt be weeping, When at some fu - ture day, I shall be far a - way, Thou shalt be weeping, Thy lone watch
wirst noch of - te um mi wei - na, Wenn i ver-gan - gen bin, Ganz weit in's Aus - land hin, Dann wirst du wei - na, Du Lie - be

keep - ing, When from my window's height, I look out on the night, I still am weep - ing, My lone watch keep - ing
lei - na Wenn I am Fen - ster steh und in die Nacht naus seh, Da muss i wei - na, Bin i al - lei - na.
keep - ing, When at some fu - ture day, I shall be far a - way, Thou shalt be weep - ing, Thy lone watch keep - ing."
klei - na, Wenn i ver - gan - gen bin, Ganz weit in's Aus - land hin, Dann wirst du wei - na Du lie - be klei - na.

3. :|: Alas! if land or sea
   Had parted him from me, :|
   I would not these sad tears be weeping
   |: But hope he'd come once more,
   And love me as before,
   And say, "cease weeping,
   Thy lone watch keeping." :|

4. |: But he is dead and gone!
   Whose heart was mine alone, :|
   And now for him I'm ever weeping;
   |: His face I ne'er shall see,
   And nought is left to me,
   But bitter weeping,
   My lone watch keeping! :|

MOORISH SERENADE.

(MAURISCHES STÄNDCHEN.)

Fr. Kücken.

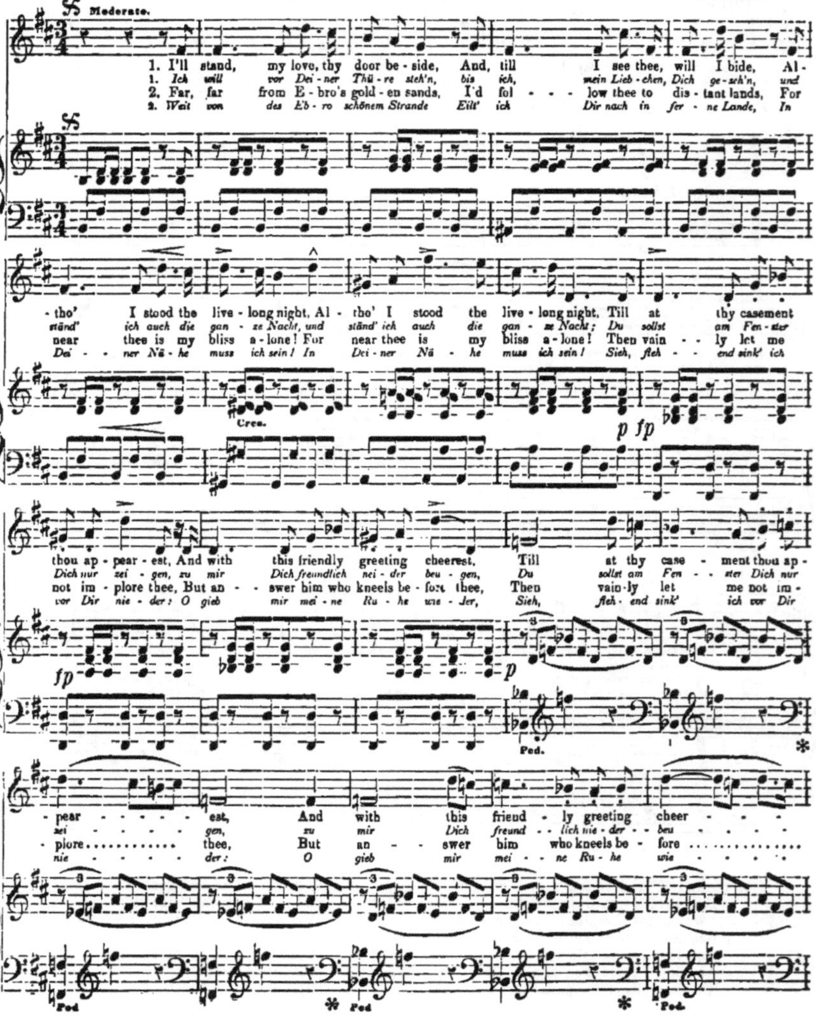

-est: "Ne'er art thou, ne'er art thou
-gen, mir sa - - - - - - gen, mir sa - - - - - - gen,
thee, "Yes, ev - - - - - - er, yes, ev - - - - - - er
-der, Und sa - - - - - - ge, und sa - - - - - - ge:
Cres.
ab - - - sent from me quite, ... ne'er ...... ab - sent
Ich ha - be Dein ge - - dacht, ... ich ...... ha - be
will I be thine own," ...... yes, ... will I
"E - - - wig bin ich Dein," ...... "ja, ... e - wig
Dim.
from me quite!"
Dein ge - - - dacht.
be thine own."
bin ich Dein."
stac.
tr
Dim.
Last time.
Ped.

THE MAY-BELLS AND THE FLOWERS.

Mendelssohn.

1. Young may-bells ring throughout the vale, And sound so sweet and clear: The

2. ℈ frost had scarce-ly ta-ken flight, When well known sounds we hear, The

dance be-gins, ye flow-ers all, Come with a mer-ry cheer. Come with a mer-ry

may-bells with re-new'd de-light, Are ring-ing doub-ly clear, Are ring-ing doub-ly

cheer. The flow-ers red, and white, and blue, mer-ri-ly flock a-round, For-

clear. Now I no more can stay at home, The may-bells call me too, The get - me - not of heav'n-ly hue, And vio - lets too a - bound, For-get-me-not of heav'nly hue, And

flow-ers to the dance all roam, Then why should I not go, The flow-ers to the dance all roam, Then

Ritar . . . . . dan . do.

Ritard.

vio - lets too a - bound, For - get - me - not of heav'n-ly hue, And vio - lets too a - bound

Ritard.

why should I not go, The flow - ers to the dance all roam, Then why should I not go.

Dim.   Ritard.

Young May-bells play a spright-ly tune, And all be - gin to dance, While o'er them smiles the

Young May-bells play a spright-ly tune, And all be - gin to dance, While o'er them smiles the

L.H.   R.H.

gen - - tle moon, With her soft sil - v'ry glance, With her soft sil - v'ry glance.

gen - - tle moon, With her soft sil - v'ry glance, With her soft sil - v'ry glance.

This Mas - ter Frost of - fen - ded sore, He in the vale ap - pear'd, Young May-bells

This Mas - ter Frost of - fen - ded sore, He in the vale ap - pear'd, Young May-bells

ring the dance no more, Gone are the flow - ers, sear'd, Gone are the flow - ers.

ring the dance no more, Gone are the flow - ers, sear'd, Gone are the flow - ers,

sear'd, The flow - ers sear'd,
But
sear'd, The flow - ers sear'd,
But
Cres - - - - - cen - - - - - do.
2nd time.
why should I not go......
Then
2nd time.
why not go The flow - ers to the dance all roam; Then
2nd time.
Cres.
why should I not go?......
why should I not ......
f

LOVING, I THINK OF THEE.

(AN ADELHEID.)

C. Krebs.

Moderato assai.
Tutti legato possibile.

1. Lov - ing, I think of thee, Shineth the sun on
1. Lie - bend gedenk ich Dein, bei'm hel - len Son - - nen-
2. Lov - ing, I think of thee, Nought can so plea - - sant
2. Lie - bend gedenk ich Dein, Nichts kann mich sonst er -

me........ ...... Or in the si - lent night,........ ... Waking from slum - bers
schein........... ein - sam in stil - ler Nacht,........ wenn ich vom Traum er
be ;........... And wheth-er joy or pain........... Vis - it my heart a -
freun ;........... E - wig in Lust und Schmerz,...... Schlägt Dir ge - treu dies'

light. Through life's event - ful sto - ry, Thine image flits be - fore me.
wacht, Auf al - len Le - bens - we - gen, lacht mir Dein Bild ent - ge - - gen,
- gain, One wish alone I cher - ish, For thee to live or per - ish!
Herz ; Mein höchster Wunsch, mein Stre - ben, Ist nur für Dich zu le - - ben,

Lov - - ing, I think of thee,   Oh could I near thee be!
Lie - - bend, gedenk' ich Dein,   O könnt ich bei Dir sein!
Lov - - ing, I think of thee,   Thou art the world to me!
Lie - - bend, gedenk' ich Dein,   Du bist mein Glück al - lein!

Through life's event - ful sto - - - ry,   Thine image flits be - fore me.
Auf al - len Le - bens - we - - - gen,   lacht mir Dein Bild ent - ge - gen,
One wish a - lone I cher - - ish,   For thee to live or per - ish!
Mein höchster Wunsch, mein Stre - - ben,   Ist nur für Dich zu le - ben,

Lov - - ing I think of thee;   Oh could I near thee be!
Lie - - bend gedenk' ich Dein,   O könnt' ich bei Dir sein!
Lov - - ing I think of thee.   Thou art the world to me!
Lie - - bend gedenk' ich Dein,   Du bist mein Glück al - lein!

(DAS ERSTE VEILCHEN.)

Mendelssohn

Andante.

mf

When the first vi - o - let spread its soft
Als ich das er - ste Veil - chen er -

bloom, How fair was its beau - ty, how sweet...... its per - fume: It breath'd but of
- blickt, Wie war ich von far - ben und duft...... ent - rückt! Die bo - tin des

p

spring - time, calm - ness and rest; Glad - ly I placed it with hope, on my
len - zes drückt ich voll lust an mei - ne schwel - len - de, hof - fen - de

p

breast, It breath'd but of spring - time, calm - ness and rest,..................... And
brust, die bo - tin des len - zes drückt ich voll lust,..................... an

p

glad - - ly I placed it with hope on my breast.
mei - - ne schwel - len - de, hof - - - - fen - - de brust.

The spring-time bath vanish'd, the vi - o - let lies
Der lenz ist vo - rü - ber, das veil - chen ist

dead,............... the vi - o - let lies dead, Buds far more bright deck its cold
todt,............... das veil - chen ist todt, rings stehn viel blu - men, blau und

bed; I heed not their beauty, in dreams still I see, I heed not their beauty, in dreams still I
roth, ich ste - he in mitten, und se - he sie kaum, ich ste - he in mitten, und se - he sie

see........ The vi - - - - - - - - - o - let, the vi - o - let, sweet
kaum,........ das veil - - - - - - chen, das veil - chen er -
pp
sf
p
hope - flow'r, that bloom'd then for me; The vi - - - - - - - - - o - let, sweet
- scheint mir in Früh - lings - traum. das veil - - - - - - - - - chen er -
pp
pp
hope - flow'r, that bloom'd then, that bloom'd then for me.
- scheint mir er - - - scheint mir in früh - lings - traum.
Ad lib.
Ped.
*
p
Dim. e Ritard.

Andantino.

1. Now the swal - lows are re - turn - ing, And the ro - - ses bloom once more; While the
1. Nun die Schwal - ben wie - der zie - hen, her zum hei - - math - lich - en Strand; und die
2. And from south - ern climes re - turn - ing, Now the swan flies to our shore, While the
2. Nun die Schwä - ne wie - der zie - hen, her zum grün - - um - flor - ten See, und die

Night - in - gale is tril - ling The glad song she sang of yore. And sweet hope is gent - ly
Ro - sen wie - der blüh - hen, auf der Hai - - de, auf dem Land! Und die Nach - ti - gal - len
ra - diant smile of spring - time, Kind - ly beams on me once more; And sweet hope, &c.
gold - nen Strah - len glü - hen, sanft her - ab aus blau - er Höh!' Dann die Hoff - nung sagt zum

whisp'ring, Deep with - in my throb - bing heart. "Soon a - gain, Thou'lt meet in gladness, Nev - er
sin - gen lieb ich in dem stil - len Hain; Ze - phyr weht auf Ro - sen Schwingen; säuseld
Her - zen, bald ver - ges - - sen ist die Pein. bald ver - schwin - - den al - le Schmerzen, bald, o

rall.

more on earth to part," "Soon a - gain, thou'lt meet in gladness, Nev - er more on earth to part."
a - ber Flur und Rain. Dort in je - - nem stil - len Hain; hof - fend, denk ich, lie - bend dein.
bald, bald bist du mein; bald ver - schwin - - den al - le Schmerzen, bald, o bald, bald bist du mein.

colla voce.

STAY WITH ME.
(BLEIB BEI MIR.)

Abt.

See the flow - ers their heads are
Wie die Blün - lein draus-sen

drooping, The gold-en Sun   is near the West...... Leave me   not   with heart des-pond - ing, Thou, my
zit - tern   in der A - bend - lüf - te Weh'n,...... und du   willst mir's Herz ver - bit - tern, und du

dear - - est, loveliest, best;   Stay with me, when all the woods are still ;   Love can shield you yet from ev' - ry
willst   schön wie - der   geh'n?   Bleib bei mir......und geh' nicht fort,   in mei'm Her-zen ist der schönste

ill,   Stay with   me when all the woods are   still ;...   Love can shield you yet from ev' - ry   ill.
Ort,   bleib bei   mir,   und geh' nicht   fort......   in mei'm Her-zen ist der schönste   Ort.

I have lov'd thee well and fond - ly, All my soul was giv'n to thee, O be - lieve that I am hap - py, Wilt thou on - ly smile on me,
Hab ge - liebt dich oh - ne En - de, hab' dir nichts zu Leid ge - than, und du drückst mir stumm die Hän - de, und du fängst zu wei - nen an!
rit.
f ten.
pp
Stay with me, when all the woods are still; Love can shield you yet from ev' - ry ill,
Wei - ne nicht . . . . . und geh' nicht fort, in mei'm Her - zen ist der schön - ste Ort
Cres.
molto riten.
Stay with me, when all the woods are still; .. Love can shield you yet from ev' - ry ill.
wei - ne nicht . . . . . . und geh nicht fort, ... in mei'm Her - zen ist der schön - ste Ort.
a Tempo.
mf

Trust not yon - - der world of sor - row, Heartless is that world and cold,...... The garb of truth may bor - row, All that glia - - tens is not gold; Stay with me, when all the woods are still; Love can shield you yet from ev' - ry ill, Stay with me when all the woods are still ;... Love can shield you yet from ev' - ry ill.

O da druss - - sen in der Fer - - ne, sind die Men - schen nicht so gut,......und ich gäb' für dich so ger - ne, ja mein Le - - ben und mein Blut. Bleib bei mir......und geh nicht fort, in mei'm Her-zen ist der schönste Ort, bleib bei mir, und geh' nicht fort...... in mei'm Her-zen ist der schönste Ort.

AWAY NOW JOYFUL RIDING.

(SPAZIEREN WOLLT ICH REITEN.)

Fr. Kücken.

Allegretto.

1. A - way now joy - ful rid - - - ing, With heart and hope so light, My foaming steed now
1. Spa - zie - ren wollt ich rei - - ten, der Lieb - sten vor die Thür, sie blickt' nach mir von
2. The trees were past us fly - - ing, The mountains seem'd to race; My heart a - lone seem'd
2. Den Zaum den ließ ich schie - - ssen, und spreng - te hin zu ihr; und that sie freud - lich

chid - - ing, Then cheer - ing his quick flight. Now! urge thee still more fleet! We'll
wei - - ten, und sprach mit gros - ser Freud'; Seht dort mein's Her - zens Zier, wie
dy - - ing, All mock'd our wea - ry pace. How slow the long hours glide; The
grü - - ssen, und sprach mit Wor - ten süss: Mein Schatz, mein höch - ste Zier, was

have a smile most sweet. Trot, trot, trot, trot, my friend - ly steed, 'Tis love and home to meet; Trot,
trabt er her zu mir! Trab, trab, trab, trab, trab, Ross - li, trab, trab, trab, trab, für und für, Trab,
road is free and wide, Trot, trot, trot, trot, a - way! a - way! We must more fleet - ly ride; Trot,
macht ihr vor der Thür, Trab, trab, trab, trab, trab, Ross - li trab, Trab, trab, trab her zu ihr, Trab,

trot, trot, trot, my friendly steed, 'Tis love and home to meet.
trab, trab, trab, trab, Ross - li, trab, Trab, trab, trab, für und für.
trot, trot, trot, a - way! a - way! We must more fleet - ly ride.
trab, trab, trab, trab, Ross - li, trab, Trab, trab, trab, her zu ihr.

THOU EVERYWHERE.
(ÜBERALL DU.)

J. Lachner.

1. O'er me night's gloo - - - - - my veil;   Waiting the day-dawn pale, I count the hours.
1. *Wenn mich der dunk - - - le Schacht*   *Schau-ri - ger Mit - ternacht ein - sam um - schliesst,*
2. Thee in the lark's . . . . clear song   I hear; Thy name at eve lulls me to rest.
2. *Weckst mich im Ler - - - chen - sang,*   *und dei - nes Namens Klang, lullt mich zur Ruh.*

Watching for morning pale, I count the hours.   Yet all is
Schau-ri - ger   Mit - ternacht ein - sam um - schliesst,   *Bin — ich doch*
At eve thy name lulls me to tran - quil rest.   Ah! ev' - ry
Und dei - nes   Na - mens Klang, lullt mich zur Ruh!   *Ach! je - nes*

bright to me,   Love, while I think of thee.   As when the shad - ows flee;
sie al - lein,   *denk, ja, Ge - lieb - te, dein,*   *die mir der Lie - - be Pein*
pic - ture fair,   Doth thy dear im - age bear.   Thou dost my soul il - lume,
süs - se Bild,   *das mir so hehr und mild,*   *Leuch - tend die see - - le füllt,*

Morn gilds the bow'rs,   Love fills my heart with bliss,   sun - - shine, and
Schmerz - lich ver - süsst,   *die mir der Lie - - be Pein*   *Schmerz - - lich ver*
O, maid most dear,   Thou dost my soul il - lume,   Maid ev - er
Theu - - re bist Du!   *Leuch - - tend die See - - le füllt,*   *Theu - - re bist*

1st. time.
flow'rs.
- süsst;
(2nd. time omit.)
mf
f
Ped.
When morn - ing shines on me, Then thy dear form I see,
Du blickst im Mor - gen - schein, bricht dann der A - bend ein,
p
In all things fair, ... In all things fair, In day's ef -
Wink'st du mir zu, ... Wink'st du mir zu. Du in des
8va
- ful - gent glow, In brooklet's tran - quil flow, In star - light, tem - pest, thou
Ta - ges Gluth, Du in des Ba - ches Fluth, Du in der Stür - me Wuth,

art ev'ry where,   Nought do I view but thee,   thee, ev'ry-
ä · · · ber · all Du!   Du in der Stür · · me Wuth,   ä · · · ber · all

- where.   dear.   Oh! maid   ev · er
Du!   Du!   O   Theu · · re bist

dear!   Oh! maid . . . .   ev · er
Du!   O   Theu . . . . re bist

dear!
Du!

THE MOORISH MINSTREL.

(DER ZIGEUNERKNABE IM NORDEN.)

Reissiger.

1. In the south of fair His-pa-nia, Where the E-bro's wa-ters foam, By the
1. *Fern im Süd' das schö-ne Spa-nien, Spa-nien ist mein Hei-math-land, wo die*
2. With my lute now long I've wan-der'd Joy-less on, from door to door, But no
2. *Und nun wand'r ich, mit der Lau-te, Traurig hier von Haus zu Haus Doch Kein*

chest-nut's verdure sha-ded, There's my birth-place and my home. On the al-mond's blushing
schat-ti-gen Ka-sta-nein rau-schen an des Eb-ro Strand. Wo die Man-deln röth-lich
friend-ly eye re-ward-ed E'er with smiles the hap-less Moor. Some with spar-ing hand, re-
hel-les Auge schaute Freundlich noch, nach mir he-raus. Spärlich reicht man mir die

Cres.

blos-soms, 'Mid the vine yards there we gaze, Where the ro-se's hue is deep-est, And the
blü-hen, wo die sheis-se Trau-be winkt, wo die Ro-sen schöner glü-hen, und das
liev-ing, Oft with an-gry words an-noy, Ne'er the bit-ter tear per-ceiv-ing, Of the
Ga-ben, Mürrisch heis-set man mich gehn. Ach! den ar-men braunen Kna-ben Will Kein

moon sheds golden rays. Where the ro-se's hue is deep-est, And the moon sheds gold-en rays
Mond-licht gold-ner blinkt, wo die Ro-sen schö-ner glü-hen und das Mondlicht gold-ner blinkt.
Moor-ish minstrel boy. Ne'er the bit-ter tear per-ceiv-ing Of the Moorish min-strel boy.
Ein-zi-ger verstehn. Ach! den ar-men braunen Kna-ben Will Kein Ein-zi-ger ver-stehn.

THE BEGGAR CHILD.

(DAS BETTELNDE KIND.)

F. Gumbert.

Andantino.

1. O you who hur - - - ry by, un - heed - - ing The beggar child's..... demure ap - peal,   Unmindful
1. Erhört des ar - - men Kin-des Bit - - te, und ge - bet mir..... ein Stückchen Brod,   auf mich ihr
   2 birds   above are sing - - ing; They know no care ....   or want on earth,   I bear their
2. weh'n   die Vöglein sin - - gen zu Gott hin - auf, ...   mit fro - hem Sinn,   die Wol - ken

of......... my earnest plead - - - ing. Could you but know   the pangs I feel,   As here for
Rei - - chen lenkt die Schrit - - te, und lin - dert ach - - die bitt - re Noth,   da - heim in
mer - - ry notes now ring - - ing So full of hap - - piness and mirth;   The clouds a -
lu - - stig vorwärts drin - - gen zum dunkeln blau - - en Him-mel hin,   mögt ihr dort

aid......... I'm in - ter - ced - - ing, Crushed down with hunger's, with hunger's heavy seal: You would not
mei - - ner nie - dern Hüt - - te, dort liegt die Mut - ter, die Mutter bleich und todt,   o hel - ft
bove......... are calmly wing - - ing To where all love..... all love and peace have birth;   Bid birds and
o - - ben Kun-de brin - - gen wie ich so ganz, so ganz ver - las - sen bin,   o grüsst mein

pass me   by   so cold.   Great la - dies glit - ter - ing   with gold!   O Father,
mir, dem ar - - men Kind,   ich bin er - starrt von Frost   und Wind,   Du gu - ter
clouds my mes - - sage bear,   I soon shall be a - far   from care: O Father, &c.
lie - bes El - - tern paar,   das mei - nes La - bens Füh - - rer war,   Du gu - ter, &c.

Cres.

Rit.
Rit.
from a world like this, Take me to thy sweet realms of
Gott send 'Ret - - - tung mir nimm' mich hin - auf, hin - auf zu
Colla parte.
Colla parte.
bliss! Oh take.............. me to thy sweet
Dir, nimm' mich.............. hin - auf, hin - -
Legato.
realms of bliss.
auf zu Dir.
1st.
The hap - py bliss.
Die Lü - fte Dir.
2nd.
8va

THE STANDARD WATCH.

(DIE FAHNENWACHT.)

P. V. Lindpaintner.

1. Where floats the stand-ard o'er the tented plain, His lonely watch the minstrel knight is keep - ing. And
1. *Der Sän - ger hält im Feld die Fahnen-wacht, In sei - nem Ar-me ruht das Schwert, das schar - fe, er*
2. The night is gone, the battle comes with day, Behold the bard. surrounding foes defy - ing; Red
2. *Die Nacht verrinnt, Kampf bringt der junge Tag, der Sän - ger will nicht von der Fah - ne wei - chen; es*

thus beguiles the time with tuneful strain, His sil - ver lute with mailed fin - ger sweep - ing. The
grüsst mit hel - lem Lied die stil - le Nacht, und spielt da - zu mit blut'ger Hand die Har - fe. Die
car - nage marks his presence in the fray, While still he sings amid the dead and dy - ing. The
blitzt sein Schwert, doch ist's ein Blitz und Schlag, und sin - gend schlägt er Le - ben - de zu Lei - chen. Die

la - dy of my love I may not name, I dare not hope my love can be re - quit - ed, Yet I will fight for
Dame, Die die ich lie - be, nenn' ich nicht, doch hab' ich ih - - re Far - ben mir er - ko - ren, ich stri - te gern für
la - dy of my love I may not name, I dare not hope my love can be re - quit - ed, Then let me die for
Da - me, die ich lie - be, nenn' ich nicht, kommt nur her - an, die Ernst mir zu durch-boh - ren; ich ster be gern für

lib - erty and fame, Be - neath the banner where my vows were plight - ed, be - neath the ban - ner where my vows were
Freiheit und für Licht, ge - treu der Fah - ne, der ich zu - ge - schwo - ren, ge - treu der Fah - ne, der ich zu - ge-

plight - ed! 3. The fight is won, death,
schwo - ren! 3. Der Tod ist satt. ge -

Molto Espressivo.

sa - ted, quits the field! Yet still the faithful bard, while life is fleet - - ing, Ex - pir - ing, lies up-
won - nen ist die Schlacht; aus tie - fen Wunden strömt des Sän - gers Le - - ben, aus sei - ner Fah - ne,

Rall.

- on his go - ry shield, This dying note with fee-ble voice re - peat - ing,
die er treu bewacht, hört man ihn sterbend noch sein Lied er - he - ben.

The lady of my love I
Die Dame, die ich lieb - te,

Dolce.   *pp*

did not name, In Heav'n a - bove, we yet may be u - nit - ed.
nannt' ich nicht, mein Le - ben ist, die Eh - re nicht ver - lo - ren!

I fought and fell for
Ich stritt, und fiel für

pp

Calando.

lib - - er - ty and fame, Be - neath the ban - ner where my vows were plight - - ed,
Frei - heit und für Licht, Ge - treu der Füh - ne, der ich zu - ge - schwo - - - - ren;

be -
ge -

Calando.

Morendo.

- neath the banner where my vows were plight - ed!
- treu der Füh - ne, der ich zu - ge - schwo - ren!

Andante.

pp

OH! WERE I BUT A MOONLIGHT'S RAY.

(O, WÄR ICH DOCH DES MONDES LICHT.)

Kücken

1. Oh, were I but a moonlight's ray, O'er flow-ers night-ly sweeping, I would in-to her

1. O, wär ich doch des Mon-des Licht! dann könnt' ich sie be-grü-ssen; ich möcht' von ih-rem

2. Oh, were I but a Night-in-gale! With tales of se-cret long-ing, Would I mak-ech-o

2. O, wär' ich eine Nach-ti-gall! Ihr wollt' ich lei-se kla-gen Der Sehnsucht Schmerz, mit

win-dow stray, And fond-ly kiss her, sleeping. She would suspect not, sweetly dreaming, The

Fen-ster nicht, und dürf-te still sie küs-sen. Tief in die Au-gen würd ich blick-en, voll

dell and vale. With lov-ing cou-ples thronging. I'd sing from deepest heart out-pour-ing The

sü-sem Schall, Nach ihrer Lie-be fra-gen. Doch säng' ich, in den heilsten Tö-nen, Die

kiss-es on her forehead streaming; Be-fore the morning's golden glow, Once on her lips I'd fondly ling'ring

rei-nem se-li-gem Ent-zü-cken, und wenn der Mor-gen wär'er-graut, dann hätt' ich sie noch ein-mal an-ge

praise of her I am a-dor-ing; And round her earthly path and mine, A wreath of song should ever light and

ho-hen Reize meiner Schönen; Ich eilt' ihr nach in Flur und Hain, Ihr könnte nah' der treue Sän-ger

glow, Be-fore the morning's gold-en flow ... Once on her lips I'd fondly ling'ring glow.

schaut, und wenn der Mor-gen wär'er-graut, dann hätt' ich sie noch ein-mal an-ge-schaut.

shine, And round her earth-ly path and mine, A wreath of song should ev-er light and shine.

sein. Ich eilt' ihr nach in Flur und Hain, Ihr könnte nah' der treue Sän-ger sein.

HYMN TO THE VIRGIN.

Song from the Lady of the Lake.

Fr. Schubert.

Very slow.

mp col Ped.

1. A - - - - ve Ma - ri - - - - a! mai - - - den
1. A - - - - ve Ma - ri - - - - a! Jung - - - frau
2. A - - - - ve Ma - ri - - - - a! un - - de
3. A - - - - ve Ma - ri - - - - a! un - - be

mild, Lis - ten to a mai - den's pray - - - er;
mild, er - hö - re ei - ner Jung - frau Fle - hen,
filed! the flin - ty couch we now must share,........... shall
flexkt! Wenn wir auf die - sem Fels hin - sin - - ken

Thou canst hear, tho' from the wild, Thou canst save........ thou canst save a
die - sem Fel - sen, starr und wild, soll mein Ge - bet zu dir hin
seem with down of ei - der piled, If thy pro - tec - tion hov - er
Schlaf, und uns dein Schutz be - deckt, wird weich der har - te Fels uns

mid . . . . des . . . pair.   Safe   may   we   sleep   beneath   thy
we . . . . . . there. . . . . hen.   Wir   schla   fen   si   cher bis   zum
there. . . . . Tho   mur   ky   cavern's   hea - vy
dün . . . . ken.   Du   lä   chelst, Ro   sendüf - t.

care, ...   Though   ban . . . ished, out - cast, and ro - viled.   O
Mor . . . gen,   ob   Men . . . schen noch   so grausam sind.
air . . . . . .   shall   breathe   of   balm if thou hast smiled ;
we . . . hen   in   die . . . ser   dump - fen Fel - sen - kluft,   O

Mai - den ! hear   a mai-den's prayer,   Moth - er, hear   a suppliant child !
Jung - frau, nich   der Jungfrau Sor - gen,   O   Mut - ter, hör   ein bit - tend Kind !
Mai - den ! hear   a mai-den's prayer,   Moth - er, list   a suppliant child !
Mut - ter, hör' des Kin - des Fle - hen,   O   Jung - frau, ei - ne Jungfrau ruft !

fp   *pp*

A . . . . ve Ma - ri . . . . . . a !
A . . . . ve Ma - ri . . . . . . a !
A . . . . ve Ma - ri . . . . . . a !
A . . . . ve Ma - ri . . . . . . a !

Dim.

FLY, BIRD OF HOPE.

(FLIEG' VÖGLEIN.)

Fr. Kücken.

Vivace.

1. Fly, Bird of hope! now fleet a - way; Thy path thou know'st full well, And
1. Flieg', Vög - lein, durch den Böh - mer - wald, so weit du kannst, in Hast, und
2. Fly! balm - y breeze! o'er wood and vale, 'Till thou love's land be near, And
2. Zieh, Lüft - chen, durch den Böh - mer - wald, und tief in's Land hin - ein, Um-

seek the home of one so dear, Where all my fond thoughts dwell. Then
setz' vor mei - nes Lieb - sten Haus, dich auf den grün - sten Ast. Und
whis - per then the sweet - est breath, Be - neath her cham - - ber dear. And
- säus - le mei - nes Lieb - sten Haus, pock' an sein Käm - - mer - lein. Und

rest ye near where she may hear, Thy song of love her heart to cheer, And
tritt er dann vor sei - ne Thür und fragt: was Vög - lein, bringst du mir! dann
ev' - ry sigh from flow - 'ret nigh, Thou'lt bid a - round her win - dow fly; And
öff - net er das Fen - ster dir und fragt: was, Lüft - chen, bringst du mir? dann

mf — **Ritenuto.** — **Poco a poco.**

thou must sing of me a - lone, And this thy bur - den dear make known; This
zwits - chre du und sei nicht bang: "O lau - - sche mild auf mei - - nen Sang, "das
they may touch her lips and say, We bear a song from love a - way, This
fäch - le du ihm Wang' und Mund, und sprich: "O wird es dir nicht kund? das

pp Molto Ritenuto.

greet - ing sweet should be ; "He loves a - lone but thee." This
ist ein Gruss von ihr, das ist ein Gruss von ihr, ein

greet - ing sweet should be ; "He loves a - lone but thee............
Gruss, ein Gruss von ihr, ein Gruss, und a - ber von ihr."

IN THE EYE THERE LIES THE HEART.

(IN DEN AUGEN LIEGT DAS HERZ.)

Franz Abt.

1. Thro' the eyes the heart doth
1. In den Au - - gen liegt das
2. What a joy one look can
2. O es ist ein lieb - lich

speak, To each look thy gaze be turn - ing. When with love thy soul is burn - ing, And
Herz, In die Au - - gen musst du se - hen Willst die Mäd - - chen du ver - ste - - hen.
give, From the eyes where love is dwell - ing. When two hearts with rap - ture swell - ing, In each
spiel, Wenn die Au - - gen sich be - lau - schen, Ih - re Bli - - cke for - schend tau - schen,

thou thy fate wouldst seek:
Wer - ben um der Lie - be Scherz.
oth - er on - ly live.
Kei - ne Re - de sagt so viel.

Rend the language of the eye,
Mer - ke wie das Au - ge spricht;
Hope with glowing tints doth shine,
Son - nen - lich - tes Far - ben - schein

There is truth in all its
Ja das Au - ge musst du
Earth to them is full of
Zeigt sich Klar dir im Ju-

glanc - es,
fra - gen,
glad - ness,
we - te,

For more truth than wisdom fan - cies,
Was mit wor - ten sie dir sa - gen,
Free from sorrow, care or sad - ness,
Far - ben uns dem Sitz der See - le!

Lo!...... within its flash - es lie.
Freund.... das ist das Rech - te nicht.
Ah!...... the light of love's di - vine.
Zeigt...... das Au - ge dir al - lein;

Thro' the
In den
Thro' the
In den

eyes the heart doth speak, To each look thy gaze be turn - ing, When with love thy soul is
Au - - gen liegt das Herz, Ja die Au - - gen musst du fra - - gen Ja die Au - - gen musst du

burn - ing; Thro' the eyes the heart doth speak.
fra - gen, In den Au - - gen liegt das Herz.

O, WERT THOU IN THE CAULD BLAST.

(DUET.)

Poetry by Robert Burns.

Mendelssohn.

Soprano 1o.

1. O wert thou in the cauld blast, On yonder lea, On yonder lea, My plaidie to the an-gry airt . . . I'd

1. O säh ich auf der haide dort Im Sturme Dich! Im Sturme dich! Mit meinem mantel vor dem Sturm Be-

Soprano 2o.

2. Or were I in the wildest waste, Sae black and bare, Sae black and bare, The des-ert were a par-a- dise, . . . If

2. O wär' ich in der Wüste, die So braun und dürr! So braun und dürr! Zum Pa-ra-die-se würde sie Wärst

Andante.

shel-ter thee, I'd shel-ter thee. Or did mis-for-tune's bit-ter storms A-round thee blaw, A-

-schütz' ich dich! Beschütz' ich dich! O wär' mit sei-nen Stür-men dir Das unglück nah, Das

thou wert there. If thou wert there, Or were I mon-arch of the globe, With thee to reign, With

du bei mir! Wärst du bei mir! Und wär ein Kö - - nig ich.. Die Er-de mein: Die

round thee blaw, Thy shield should be my bo - som, To share it a', To share it a'.

un-glück nah, Dann wär' dies herz dein Zufluchts-ort; Gern theilt ich's ja! Gern theilt ich's ja!

thee to reign, The bright-est jew-el in my crown, Wad be my Queen, Wad be my Queen.

Er-de mein Du wärst in mei-ner krone doch Der schön-ste Stein! Der schön-ste Stein!

FROM THE ALPS THE HORN RESOUNDIN c.

(DAS ALPEN HORN.)　　　　　Proch.

From the Alps the horn re - sound-ing, With its tones so soft, so clear, From the earth with bliss en -
Von der Al - pe tönt das Horn, gar so zaub'risch, wun - der - bar, 'sist doch ei - ne eig'ne

chant'-ing. Wafts my soul to heaven near. Other skies with mild - ness beam - ing, To my
Lust, wiht' dem Him - mel schon für - wahr. And're Blu - men, and're Wol - ken, wie in

mind bring no re - lief: Tho' I fly there's no es-cap - ing From the an - - guish of my
ei - nem Zauber - reich, nur mein Lie - ben, nur mein Lie - ben bleibt sich e - - - - wig, e - wig

grief. To the dark and gloomy Alps, Here I come to leave my pain: But 'tis
gleich, und ich zieh' zur Al - pe hin, will dem eig' - - - nen Schmerz entflieh'n; doch ich

use - - less, for I feel, That my thoughts with thee remain. But 'tis use - - - less, for I
denk' an Dich zu - rück, muss wohl wei - - ter, wei - ter zieh'n; . doch ich d-nk' an Dich zu-

feel, That my thoughts with thee re - main. And the mel - - o - dy so
rück, muss wohl wei - - ter, wei - ter zieh'n. Und die trü - - ben Mel o -

mourn - ful Must, a - las! my emblem be, For the bliss, I am in search of, I can
die - en, drin - gen in die See - le mir, denn das Glück, das fern ich su - cir, find' ich

find a - lone with thee, For the bliss I am in search of, I can find a-lone with
e - - wig nur bei dir; und das Glück das fern'ich su - che, find' ich e - - wig nur bei

thee.   For the bliss   I am in   search of, I   can   find   a-lone with   thee.
Dir ;   und das Glück   das fern' ich   su . che, find' ich   e - - wig nur bei   Dir !

O THANK ME NOT.

Words by Müller.   (WIDMUNG.)   R. Franz.

O   thank me   not, tho' sweet the   mu - sic ;   Mine to   en -
dan - ke   nicht   für   die - se   Lie - der,   Mir   ziemt   es

- joy. the praise be   thine,   From thee it   came ;   I but re - turn thee What
dank - bar dir   zu   sein ;   Du gabst sie   mir ;   Ich ge - be   wie - der, Was

thou hast giv'r, it was not mine. When thy dear
jetzt und einst und e - wig dein. Lein sind sie

eyes with lov - ing ra - aiance. On me threw rays of soft - est light,
ul le ja ge - we - sen, Aus dei - - ner lie - bcn Au - gen Licht,

Plain - ly I read there these fair ver - ses, Know - est thou not the
Hab' ich sie treu - lich ab - ge - le - sen, Kennst du die eig - nen

song is thine? Know - est thou not the song is thine?
Lie - der nicht? Kennst du die eig - - nen Lie - der nicht?

THE PASSAGE BIRD'S FAREWELL.

Mendelssohn

Andante Sostenuto.

1. Ah, once how fair...... both wood and lawn, But now so dull...... the world has
2. birds,...... our sorrow's come; The leaves are gone,........ we have no

1. Ah, once how fair...... both wood and lawn, But now so dull........ the world has

grown! 'Tis gone, the joy - ous sum-mer time, And sor - ry win - ter sends its rime,...... 'Tis gone, the
home; To seek one 'neath a warm-er sky, We far a - way from here must fly,...... We far a -

grown! 'Tis gone, the joy - ous sum - mer time, And sor - ry win - ter sends its rime,...... 'Tis gone, the

Coda to 2d verse.

joy - ous sum - mer time,...................... And sor - ry win - ter sends his rime.
way from here must fly,...................... To seek a home 'neath warm-er sky, We far a

joy - ous sum - mer time,...................... And sor - ry win - ter sends his rime.

Cres.

Cres.

Cres.

Fine.
way from here must fly........
With verdant shel - ter every where we knew not
Fine.
Dim.
p
The sun shone clear, we sang a - way In mirth and joy the live - long
sad - ness, had no care, The sun shone clear, we sang a - way In mirth and joy the live - long
day, In mirth and joy the livelong day........ Now we poor
Cres.
day, The sun shone clear, we sang a - way, Now we poor
Cres.
p

MOTHER, OH! SING ME TO REST.

(MUTTER, O SING' MICH ZUR RUH!)

R. Franz.

Andantino Simplice.

1. Moth-er! oh, sing me to rest, As in my bright days de - part - - - ed.
1. Mut - ter, o sing' mich zur Ruh', Wie auch in schö - ren Stun - - - den.

Sing to thy child, the sick - heart - - ed, Songs for a spir - it op - press'd
Sing' meinem Her - zen, dem wun - - - - den, Trö - sten - de Lie - der sing' Du.

Lay this tired head on thy breast!
Drü - cke die Au - gen mir zu!

Flowers from the night - dew are clos - - - - ing, Pil - grims and mourners re -
Blu - men die Häup - ter jetzt nei - - - - gen; Trau - ern - de ras - ten und

pos - - - - - ing,   Moth - er, oh!   sing   me   to   rest!
schwei - - - - *gen,*   *Mut - ter, o   sing' mich zur Ruh!*

mf   Dim.

Take back thy   bird to   its   nest!
Bit - te dein Vö - gel - chen   Da!

p

Wea - ry is   young life when   blight - - - ed,   Heav - y   this   love un - re -
Stür - me, ach! ha - ben's ent - fie - - - dert: *Lie - be, sie   drückt un - er -*

mf

pp Poco riten.

quit - - - ed,   Moth - er, oh!   sing me   to   rest! . . . .
wie - - - dert; *Mut - ter, o   sing' mich zur Ruh'! . . . .*

Poco riten.   Un poco riten.

Dim.   *pp*

THE WILD ROSEBUD.

Words by Goethe.   (HEIDEN-RÖSLEIN.)   F. Schubert.

1. Once a boy a rose es-pied, Blooming in the wild-wood; Blushing on the
1. Sah ein Knab ein Rös-lein stehn, Rös-lein auf der Hei - den, war so jung und
2. Said the boy. "I long to break Ro-se-bud of the wild-wood." Rose-bud answer'd.
2. Kna-be sprach "Ich bre-che dich, Rös-lein auf der Hei - den." Rös-lein sprach; "Ich

thick-et side, Ho, its dain-ty bud descried, With the glee of child-hood.
mor-gen-schön, lief er schnell es nah zu sehn, sah's mit vie-len Freu-den.
"If you break, I my own de-fence must take, 'Gainst the pranks of child-hood.
ste-che dich, dass du e-wig denkst an mich, und ich will's nicht lei - - den."

Cres.

Ro-sy, ro-sy, ro-sy bud, Rose-bud of the wild-wood!
Rös-lein, Rös-lein, Rös-lein roth, Rös-lein auf der Hei - - den!

3 But the boy would fain possess,
Rosebud from the wildwood;
But as from the stalk 'twas torn,
Pricked him deep the cruel thorn,
Little grief of childhood!
Rosy, rosy, rosy bud,
Rosebud of the wildwood!

3 Und der wilde Knabe brach,
Röslein auf der Heiden,
Röslein wehrte sich und stach,
Half ihr doch kein weh und ach,
Musst es eben leiden!
Röslein, Röslein, Röslein roth,
Röslein auf der Heiden.

Schubert.

1. A - dieu! 'tis love's last greet-ing, The part - ing hour is come! And
2. A - dieu! go thou be - fore me, To join the ser - aph throng! A

fast thy soul is fleeting, To seek its star - ry home! Yet dare I mourn when
se - cret sense comes o'er me I tar - ry here not long! A - dieu! there comes a

Heaven Has bid thy soul be free, A life of bliss has giv - en For
morrow, To ev' - ry day of pain! On earth we part in sor - row, To

ev - ermore to thee! Yet dare I mourn when Heaven Has bid thy soul be
meet in bliss a - gain! A - dieu! there comes a morrow, To ev' - ry day of

free,   A fresh - er life has giv - en   For all   e - ter - ni -
pain;   On earth   we part   in sor - row,   To meet   in bliss a -

- ty.
- gain.

WE MET BY CHANCE.

F. Kucken.

1. When even - ing brings the
2. Once, how   I cannot
3. The ro - ses, when the

Allegretto.

Sf   Legato.

twilight hour, I   pass a lone - ly   spot,   Where oft   she comes to   cull the flower   We
well divine, Un - less by chance, we   kissed;   I   found   her lips were close to mine,   So
zephyrs woo Im - part what they re - ceive;   They   sigh   and sip the   balmy dew,   But

call   " For - get - me - not."   She nev - er whis - pers go, nor stay,   She
I   could not re - sist;   As nei - ther whis - per'd yea, nor nay,   As
nev - - er whis - per give!   Our love is mu - tual, this we know,   Our

Ritard.   A Tempo.

nev - - er whis - pers go,   nor stay; · · · ·   We   met   by chance,   the usu - al way,   We
nei - ther whis - per'd yea, nor nay, · · ·   They met by chance,   the usu - al way,   They
love is mu - tual, this we know · · · ·   Though nei - ther tells   the oth - er so,   Though

met by chance, the usu - al   way,   We   met   by chance,   we met   by chance, We
met by chance, the usu - al   way,   They   met   by chance,   they met   by chance, They
nei - ther tells   the oth - er   so,   Our   love is mu - - - tual, this   we know, Though

met   by chance, the usu - al   way.
met   by chance, the usu - al   way.
nei - ther tells   the oth - er   so.

THE HERDSMAN'S MOUNTAIN HOME.
(DER SCHWEIZERBUE.)

F. Abt.

Moderately quick.

1. On the mountain steep and hoary, Sounds the Herdsman ev'ning song; Where the clouds, in golden glo-ry, Float the
1. *Auf der Al - ma heit - ren Hö - hen klingt des Sen - nen A - bend - lied, Wol - ken kom - men, Wol - ken ge - hen, hell, vom*
2. Where the al - pine rose is blowing, There the Herdsman builds his home; From his couch at morning going, With the
2. *Auf der Al - ma stol - zen Ber - gen, baut der Sen - ne sich ein Haus! früh am Mor - gen mit den Ler - chen geht er*

ambient tide a - long; Where the clouds in gold-en glo - ry Float the ambient tide a - long! La la
A - bendschein be - glüht, Wol - ken kom - men, Wol - ken ge - hen, hell, vom A - bendschein be - glüht. La la
lark be loves to roam : From his couch at morn-ing go - ing, With the lark he loves to roam! La la
an sein Werk hin - aus. früh am Mor - gen, mit den Ler - chen, geht er an sein Werk hin - aus. La la

la................. la la la la la la la la la.... With the la la la................. la la
la................. la la la la la la la la la.... With the la la la................. la la

la la la la la la la!
La la la la la la la.

HOW CAN I LEAVE THEE?

Cramer.

Andante ma non troppo.

1. How can I leave thee, Queen of my lov-ing heart? Dear - er to
2. Blue is the sweet flow'r They call "for - get-me-not," That flow'r place
3. Were I a bird, love, I'd soon re - turn to thee, Nor hawk's nor

me thou art Than light and life. This heart and soul of mine,
on thy breast, And think on me; Should flower and hope both fade,
fal - con's beak Should stay my flight; Fate may some ar - row send,

So close are knit to thine, That I can soon - er life Than thee re - sign.
Yet will our love live on, All else may die, but love We'll ne'er re - sign.
Dy - - ing I fly to thee, Bless'd with one look of thine, I life re - sign

LA SERENADE.

Schubert.

1. Thro' the leave the night-winds moving, Mur - mur low and
2. Moonlight on the earth is sleep - ing, Winds are rustling

sweet ; To thy cham - ber window rov - ing, Love hath led my feet.
low. Where the darkling streams are creep - ing, Dearest let us go.

Si - lent prayers of blissful feel - ing, Link us tho' a - part, Link us tho' a -
All the stars keep watch in heav - en, While I sing to thee, While I sing to

part, On the breath of mu - sic stealing, To thy dreaming heart, To thy dreaming heart.
thee ; And the night for love was giv - en, Dearest come to me, Dearest come to me.

Sad - ly in the for - est mourning, Wails the whippoorwill, And the heart for thee is yearning,

Bid it love, be still, Bid it love, be still,..... Bid it

love, be still.

PEACE OF MIND.

(SEELENFRIEDE.)

H. A. Sponholtz.

Peace - ful, si - lent, hap - py hour,   O'er me throw thy spells of pow'r!   In the wood,   the birds at
Stil - le, si - sse, sel' - ge Ruh',   schliess du mir die Au - gen zu,   Wie im Wald   das Vö - ge -

rest.   Gently   rock   me on thy breast!   Gently rock   me on thy breast,
- lein,   wie - ge   du   mich se - lig ein,   wie - ge   du   mich se - lig ein.

Glad - ly day has shed its light,   Glad - ly comes the peaceful night ;   And the
Hei - ter ist der Tag voll - bracht,   hei - ter kommt die kla - re Nacht,   und die

might- y star- ry world, Has its ma- jes- ty, un- furl'd. Has its
gro- sse Ster- nen- schaar, glänzt am Him- mel wun- der- bar, glänzt am

ma- jes- ty un- furl'd. O'er the planets, as they roll,
Him- mel wun- der- bar. U- ber Sterne, ü- ber'm Mond,

Rules the God who rules the soul, O'er me, Lord, thy vi- gils keep! Let thy
Gott, der mir im Her- zen wohnt, hal- te du, Herr, die- se Nacht, ü- ber

child in safe- ty sleep! Let thy child in safe- ty sleep!
dei- nem Kind die Wacht, ü- ber dei- nem Kind die Wacht,

'TWAS EVENING; AT THE WINDOW.

(ERINNERUNG.)

Graben Hoffmann.

Andante Con Moto.

1. 'Twas eve-ning; at the win - dow Were we,— my Love and I. I
1. Wir sa - ssen still am Fen - - ster; das Licht war aus ge - löscht, ihr

Piu Moto.

heard her dear heart beat - ing, I heard her gent - ly sigh; ... And, with my arm a -
Herz - chen hört ich schla - gen, sie drück - te mir die Hand; ... sie schmieg - te, tief er -

Rall. 1st.

- round her, Her head up - on my breast, ... She wept, for love, for sor - row, With
- grif - fen, sich stumm an mei - ne Brust, in rü - sser Weh - muth beb - - ten wir

A Tempo.

sad' - ning fears op - press'd, And sor - - row, With sad' - ning fears op - pressed.
träu - mend un - be - wusst, sie beb - - ten wir träu - mend un - be - wusst.

Colla voce.

2. She wept, and said so soft - - ly, With blush - ing cheeks the while, "For -
2. Da wein - te sie, und fleh - - te mit glü - hen - dem Ge - sicht; Ver -
3. A - las! for those fond mo - ments Of love, of pain, and joy, Long
3. Wo - hin sind je - - ne Ta - - ge der sü - ssen Lie - bes - lust, mein

- get me not, thy dear - est, Let none thy heart be - guile, For I an or - phan
- giss auch in der Fer - ne Dein treu - es Mäd - chen nicht; ich steh' al - lein auf
past, now old, fond me - mo - ry Will oft the hours em - ploy; Long since hath she her
Haar ist längst er - grau - t, er - kal - tet mei - ne Brust; sie hat den Va - ter

Piu Moto.

maid - - en Live but for thee a - lone; Thou art as fa - ther, moth - er, Thou
Er - - den, mein Hof - fen lebt in Dir, Du bist mein Va - ter, Mut - ter, Du
fa - - ther Re - join'd, where an - gels dwell, With Moth - er Earth she slum - bers, In
fun - - den, in stil - ler Him - mels - ruh. und Mut - ter Erd', die küh - - le, deckt

Rall. 1st.

A Tempo. **2nd.**

art my on - ly one, For moth - - er, Thou art my on - ly one!"
bist mein Al - les mir, ich Mut - - ter, Du bist mein Al - les mir.
yon - der flow'- ry dell, Long slum - bers, In yon - der flow'- ry dell.
sanft die Toch - ter zu, sie küh - - le, deckt sanft die Toch - ter zu.

Colla voce. **Fine.**

BRIGHT STAR THAT CROWNS WITH BEAUTY.
(DU KLEINES BLITZENDES STERNELEIN.)

Fr. Kücken.

Moderato.

1. Bright star, that crowns with beau - - ty The realms for which you glow,...... Thou
1. Du klei - nes blit - zen - des Ster - ne - lein, nun sa - ge mir, was willst du?...... du

canst but shine a - bove, me, Why fond - ly gaze be - low;...... Thou
kannst da o - ben ja se - lig sein, was blinzelst du mir denn zu?...... du

canst but shine a - bove, me, Why fond - ly gaze be - low?...... Bright
kannst da o - ben ja se - lig sein, was blinzelst du mir denn zu?...... Du

star, that crowns with beau - - ty, The realms for which you glow, Thou canst but
klei - nes blitzen - des Ster - ne - lein, nun sa - ge, was willst denn du? du kannst ja dort

ten.
A Tempo.
Poco Ritard.
shine a - bove . . . me, ... Why fond - ly gaze be - low?
o - - ben se - - lig sein, ... ja se - - lig, se - lig sein.
do.
Ritard.
Svolvez. Rit.
Ped.
A Tempo.
Espress.
Thy
Such'
Espress.
A Tempo.
Riten.
Dolce.
twin star in the heav - - ens Seek thou, and hap - py be, ... The
du dir dein Liebchen im Ster - nen - schein, und lass mich mit Blin - zeln in Ruh,' . . . . ich
Piu Animato.
Cres.
earth - ly star I wor - - ship, Is love - lier far than thee . . . . The
hab' auf Er - den ein Ster - - ne - lein, das ist viel schö - ner als du! . . . . ich

earth - ly star I wor - - ship. Is love - lier far than thee. . . . . Bright
hab' auf Er - den ein Ster - ne - lein, das ist viel schö - ner als du! . . . . Du

star that shines a - bove. . . . me, Thou there mayst hap - - py be. The earth - ly
kői - - nes bli tzen des Ster - ne - lein, o kiss, o lass mich in Ruh! ich hab' auf

star I wor - - ship, Is love - lier far . . . . than thee, The earth - ly star I wor -
Er - den ein Ster - ne - lein, das ist viel schö - - - ner als du, ich hab' auf Erden ein Ster - ne -

- ship . . . . . . Is love - lier than thee . . . . Far love - lier than thee.
- lein . . . . viel schö - - ner als du, viel schö - ner als du!

THE DARK EYE.
(BITTE.)

Words by Lenau.   R. Franz.

Larghetto Sostenuto.

On me turn thy spark-ling lus-tre, Dark eye, filled with gen - tle light,
Weil' auf mir, du dunk-les Au-ge, Ue-be dei - ne gan - ze Macht,

Ear - nest, mild, with dream-light beam-ing, Fair as day, and calm as night!
Ern - ste, mil - de, träu - me - ri - sche, Un - er - gründ - lich sü - sse Nacht.

With thy pow'r of blest en - chant-ment, Take me from this world a - way;
Nimm mit dei - nem Zau - ber - dun - kel Die - se Welt von hin - nen mir,

Rule my life, and rule for-ev - er, Thee a - lone, will I o - bey.
Dass du ü - ber mei - nem Le - ben Ein - sam schwe - best für und für.

THOU ART GONE FAR, FAR AWAY.

(SCHEIDEN UND LEIDEN.)

Hieron Truhn.

1. Thou art gone, far, far a - way, and friends thou'rt not with me; Yet
1. Und bist Du fern, und bist Du weit, und zürnst noch im - mer mir! Doch
2. Full was the world of ro - ses fine, when I with thee did roam; And
2. Wie stand die Welt voll Ro - sen schön, da ich bei Dir noch war. da

mourn - ful - ly, by night and day, my thoughts are still with thee; I
Tag und Nacht, voll Trau - rig - keit, ist all' mein Sinn bei Dir. Ich
ev' - ry - where the bright moonshine dis - pell'd the com - ing gloom;
rauscht' es grün von al - len Höh'n, da schien der Mond so klar.

think of thine eyes, thine eyes so blue, and of thy heart so true. Ah!
denk' an Di - ne Au - gen blau, und an Dein Herz da - zu. ach,
Thou gav'st a rose, and I kiss'd thee, I kiss'd and sung to thee. Ah!
Du brachst die Ros', ich küss - te Dich, ich küsst' und sang da - zu; Wohl

no one, no one can there be, whom I could love like thee! Ah!
Kei - ne, Kei - ne find ich je, die so mich liebt, wie Du! ach

no one, no   one   can   there be, whom I could love like thee!
Kei - ne, Kei - ne find' ich je,   die so mich lieb, wie Du!

2. Now have I   free-dom,   as   a   bird that o - ver the   moun - tain flies;
2. Wohl bin ich frei nun,   wie   der Falk', der ü - ber die   Ber - ge fliegt;

For   whom the world, the beau - teous world, clear,
vor   dem die Welt, die schö - ne Welt, hell

bright and o - pen lies;   Yet has the bird   its   home - ly nest,
son - nig of - fen liegt;   doch hat der Falk' sein   hei - misch Nest,

Più moto e con passione.
but where can I find rest?......... Ah? no one, no one
und wo find ich einst Ruh?........... Ach Kei - - ne, Kei - ne
Più moto e con passione.
fp
f
can there be, whom I could love like thee.......... Ah! no one, no one
find' ich je, die so mich liebt' wie Du!............ ach Kei - ne, Kei - ne
p
p
rfz
sfz
Vibrato.
can there be, whom I could love like thee!
find' ich je, die so mich liebt' wie Du!
fp
rfz
rfz
f
p
p
p
ritard.
rfz
Un poco Lento.
Sad was the day, sad was the hour, the hour that part - ed us, When
O schlimmer Tag, O schlimme Stund', die uns für im - mer schied; da
p
p
pp
pp
Marcato.

from my heart's deep-est core de-part-ed peace and bliss;
sind aus mei-nes Her-zens Grund ge-schie-den Freud' und Fried.

Now seek I thee o'er land and sea, no rest nor peace for me; For
Nun such' ich wohl durch Land und See, und ha-be nicht Rast noch Ruh; denn

Piu lento e con molto anima.

no one, no one can there be, whom I could love like thee! Ah!
Kei-ne, Kei-ne find' ich je, die so mich liebt' wie Du! ach

no one, no one can there be, whom I could love like thee!
Kei-ne, Kei-ne find' ich je, die so mich liebt, wie Du!

Fine.

THOU ART SO NEAR AND YET SO FAR.

A. Reichardt.

1. I know an eye, so soft-ly bright, That glistens like a star of night; My soul it
2. That eye so soft as violets blue, A treas-ure bears of morning dew; And when its

draws with glances kind To heav'n's blue vault, and there I find An-oth-er star as pure and
light entranced I see, What joy, what pain pos-ses-ses me! A world where I would gladly

clear, As that which mildly sparkles here. Be-lov-ed eye, be-lov-ed star, Thou art so
dwell Is that bright orb, I love so well. Be-lov-ed eye, be-lov-ed star, Thou art so

near, and yet so far. Belov-ed eye, be-lov-ed star, Thou art so near, and yet so far.

If closed at last that ra - diant eye should be, No more the day.... will dawn for me; If night should

lim it laugh - ing light, Oh then for ev - - er ev - er 'twill be night. Those eyes that

bright - - ly softly shine For me the Sun and Moon com-bine Beloved eye. be-lov-ed star, Thou art so

near and yet so far. Be-lov-ed eye, be-lov-ed star, Thou art so near and yet so far.

HEAR'ST THOU NOT.

Words by Eichendorff.

J. Dessauer.

Andante.

1. Hear'st thou not the trees soft murm – ring, Soft – ly whisp – 'ring through the night?
1. Hörst du nicht die Bäu – me rau – schen draus – sen durch die stil – le Rund'?
2. Know – est thou the wondrous lo – gends Framed in many an an – cient rhyme?
2. Kennst du noch die ir – ren Lie – der aus der al – ten schö – nen Zeit?

Hear'st thou not the brooklet rip – – – pling, Wondrous fair in calm moon-light? . . . .
Lockt's dich nicht hinab zu lau – – – schen von dem Söller in dem Grund,
They awak – en throng,ing fan – – – cies, Visions of the old – en time, ...
Sie erwa – chen al – le wie – – – der, Nachts, in Waldeein – sam – keit, ...

Art thou not im – pelled to wan – der Slow a – long yon tran – quil stream, Where, re – flected, towers,
wo die vie – len Bä – che ge – hen von – der – bar in Mon – den – schein, und die stil – len Schlösser
When, as now, the woods were whispering, Zeph – yrs breathed of fra – grance full,
wenn die Bäu – me träu – mend lau – schen und der Flie – der duf – tet schwül,

cas – – – tles, Lie like pic – tures of . . . . a dream.
se – – – hen in den Fluss vom ho – – – hen Stein.

Nymphs from sparkling waters ris - - - - ing;— Come away, so calm, so cool; Come..... the
und im Fluss die Rixen rau - - - schen, komm herab, hier ist's so kühl, komm'..... her -

night ... is calm and cool, come... the night...... is
- ab,...... hier ist's so kühl, komm'.... her - - ab........... hier

calm and cool. come........ the night is calm, is
ist's so kühl, komm'........ her - ab, hier ist's so

cool,......... so calm, so cool !......
kühl,......... hier ist's so kühl.

LEAVES ARE FALLING, FALLING EVER.

(BLÄTTER LÄSST DIE BLUME FALLEN.)

R. Franz.

Leaves are falling, falling ev - er; From my loved one I must sever, Ah! sweet dove, my dear - est,

Blät - ter lässt die Blu - me fal - len. Und von Liebchen muss ich wal - len. Gott mit dir du klei - nes,

Ah! sweet dove, my dear - est, God be with you.

Gott mit dir du fei - nes, sü - sses Täub - chen.

Yel - low moonlight on the meadow, Pale we stand in th'willow's shadow. Oh! sweet dove, my near - est,

Gelb steigt auf der Mond der Haide, Wir sind blass auch al - le bei - de. Gott mit dir, du klei - nes,

Ah! sweet dove, my dear - est, God be with you.

Gott mit dir, du fei - nes, sü - sses Täub - chen.

Dew falls on the leaves from heaven, To our eyes no tears are giv-en. Ah! sweet dove, my dear - est,
Thau fällt auf den Ast, der trocken, Uns im Aug' die Thränen stocken. Gott mit dir, du klei - nes,

Ah! sweet dove, my dear - est, God be with you!
Gott mit dir, du fei - nes, sü - sses Täub - chen.

Ros - es fragrant, joy-ous greeting, Glad foretell our hap-py meeting. Ah! sweet dove, my near - - est,
Blü - hen Ros - en frisch und Flie - der, Dann wohl seh - en wir uns wie - der. Gott mit dir du klei - nes,

Ah! sweet dove, my dear - - - est, God be with you.
Gott mit dir, du fei - - nes, sü - sses Täub - - chen.

THE THREE STUDENTS.

(DIE DREI LIEBCHEN.)

W. Speier.

Allegretto e piacevole.

1. Three gal - lant youths were sit - ting hard by the no - ble Rhine,
1. Drei mun - tre Bur - schen sas - - sen ge - müth - lich bei dem Wein,

And free - ly fill'd their glass - es with heart in - spiring wine, with heart in -
und schenkten ihn gar wac - ker in ih - re Glä - ser ein, in ih - re

- spiring wine. And fill'd their glasses with heart cheering wine.
Glä - ser ein. und schenkten ihn in ih - re Glä - ser ein.

Piu Moderato. *Andante.*

1. Then out spoke Leuthold, "Let the gob - lets high be crown'd! I have at home a
1. Da sp--ach der Eine:" Füllet die Be - cher bis zum Rand! Ich hab' zu Haus ein
2. "Now then for mine.' said Ludwig. "I too a love can boast, For whose dear name I
2. Nun dean! es rief der Zweite, auch ich be - sitz ein Lieb, mit den ich schäckernd

lov'd one, to her the toast go round; With black eyes and with ra - ven locks,
Lieb - - chen, dem sei mein Gruss ge - sandt; Schwarz - au - gig und schwarz - lo - - - ckig,
chal - lenge th'en - thu - si - as - tic toast. With ha - zel eyes and au - burn locks,
manch - mal mir schon die Zeit ver - trieb; Braun - au - gig und braun - lo - - - ckig,

State - ly as mountain pine, state - ly as mountain pine, And lips so freshly
wie ei - ne Tan - ne schlank, wie ei - ne Tan - ne schlank, und Lippen glühend
Light stepp'd as bounding deer, light stepp'd as bounding deer, With silv'ry voice like
leichtschreitend wei ein Reh, leichtschreitend wei ein Reh, und ih - re Stimme

glow - ing, whose nec - tar all is mine. whose nec - tar all is
fri - sche, wo man - chen Rausch-ich trank, wo man - chen Rausch-ich
matin bell, on moun - tain sounding clear. on moun - tain sounding
rei - ner, wei Glock auf Ber - ges - höh', wie Glock auf Ber - ges -

mine, whose nec - tar all is mine." Then clash'd their meeting glass - es, and gave a good - ly
trank, wo man - chen Rausch-ich trank. Da tra - fen sich die Glä - ser und ga - ben gu - ten
clear, on mountain sounding clear." Then clash'd a - gain their glass - es, and gave a good - ly
- höh', wie Glock auf Ber - ges - höh'. Da tra - fen sich die Glä - ser und ga - ben gu - ten

Tempo primo.
L'istesso Movimento.
clang, Whose spirit note e - lec - tric, a - far thro' e - ther rang,
Klang, es möchte fernhin tö - nen wie grüssen - der Ge - - sang,
Ped.
a - far through e - ther rang. a - far through e - ther rang.
wie grüs - - sen - der Ge - sang, wie grüs - - sen - der Ge - sang.
Moderato.
"Hah!" Leutbold cried, "by that mag - ic sign the kiss. I trow, I gave Christine at part - ing, her
Ei! sprach der Er - ste wie - der, dies deut' ich mir schon gut! Mein Liebchen denkt jetzt mei - ner und
Quoth Ludwig. "by that to - ken, my part - ing song I trow, That late I breath'd to Ber - tha, her
Da rief der Zweit' in Freu - den, dies Klin - gen ist mir werth, sie singt jetzt wohl das Lie - lein, das
p
Piu Crescendo.
lips are tasting now. her lips are tasting now, her lips are tast - ing now!"
uns - - re Küsse Gluth, und unsrer Küsse Gluth, und unsrer Küs - se Gluth!
sweet lips are warbling now, my parting song, I trow. her lips are warbling now!"
scheidend ich sie ge - lehrt, dies Klingen ist mir werth, dies Klingen ist mir werth!
Piu Crescendo.
f
p

Più Moderato.

"I too," quoth high born Heinrich,   "I know a gen - tle maid,   To   her my troth is
Auch ich sprach leis' der Dritte,   ich weiss wohl ei - ne Magd;   wir   lie - ben uns so

f p   p

Ritard.   Andante.   Ped.

plight - - ed, my   ho - liest ho - mage paid;   With a - zure eyes and gold - en locks,
treu - lich in al - le E - - wig - keit.   blau - aug - ig und blond - lo - - ckig,

Ped.   Ped.   Ped.

mild as the morn in May,   mild as the morn in May,   Her ev'ry word and
mild wie der Son - ne Licht,   mild wie der Son - ne Licht,   ich kann es nicht be -

Allegretto.
2/4

p   p

mo - tion an   an - gel's heart be - tray,   an an - gel's heart be -
- schrei - ben dies En - gels - an - ge - sicht,   dies En - gels - an - ge -

p

Ad lib.

- tray, an on-gel's heart be - tray. Then clash'd a - gain their glasses, when Heinrich's burst in
-sicht, dies En-gels-an-ge- sicht. Da tra-fen sich die Gläser, des Drit-ten Glas zer-

8va.

p *f* Ped.

Recit. Andante.

twain! A pierc-ing shriek! long trembling, far spread that cry of pain! Too well the comrades
-sprang! Ein Schmer-zens-ruf! Lang zitternd und gel-lend war der Klang. Die bei-den Er-sten

ff Tremolo. *ff* *pp*

Ped. Ped.

Con Molto Express.

read the sign, si - lent gloom pre - vail'd, While Heinrich, pierc'd with an - guish, his fond hopes
schau-ten ernst, schweigend hin vor sich, der Drit-te a-ber wein-te, wein-te viel

ff

Largo. Sempre Dolce.

blighted, bit - ter - ly bewail'd! At that same hour, far
Thränen, wein-te bitterlich! Und zu dersel - ben

pp *pp*

Ped. Ben marcato il basso.

dis - tant, a peaceful vale with-in, The summoning bell was bid - ding the solemn rites be - gin. But
Stun - de, in fer - nem Hei - mathsthal, da tönten wie Himmels - grü - sse die Glo - cken im Cho - ral. Nur

one there was whose dull ear such sounds shall hear no more, She slumber'd so still and peaceful, she slumber'd so still and
ei - ne Einz'ge hör - te die from - men Klänge nicht; die schlummerte still und friedlich, die schlummerte still und

peaceful, the an - gel form'd Le - nore.   Her mild blue eyes were ray - less, tho
fried - lich, ein En - gelsan - ge - sicht.   Die mil - den blau - en Au - gen, die

palsied lids be - neath,   And mid those golden tress - es, there lay, there lay a funer - al wreath.
wur - en oh - ne Glanz, und in den blon - den Lo - cken, da lag, da lag ein Tod - ten - kranz.

Words by Heine.   (AM MEER.)   **F. Schubert.**

Adagio assai.

Be - neath the ev' - ning's last sweet smile, The sea far out was shin - ing; We
Das Meer er - glänz - te weit hin - aus* im letz - ten A - bend - schei - - ne, wir

Molto Legato.

sat beside the lone beach house, And watch'd the sun's declin - ing. The
sus - sen am ein - sa-men Fi - scherhaus, wir sas - sen stumm und al - lei - ne. Der

clouds came on, the wa - ters rose, And loud - - ly the sea - bird was
Ne - bel stieg, das Was - ser schwoll, die Mö - - ve flog hin und

call - - ing! And from thine eyes the ten - der tears, In gen - tle drops were fall - ing.
wie - - der; aus dei - nen Au - gen, lie - be - voll, fie - len die Thrä - nen nie - - der.

I saw them fall up - - on thy hand, And down - wards low - ly bend - - ing, I
Ich sah sie fal - len auf dei - ne Hand, und bin aufs Knie ge - - sun - - ken, ich
pp
kiss'd them off, my own dim eyes With ri - sing tears con - tend - ing. And
hab' von dei - ner weis - sen Hand die Thrä - nen fort - ge - - trun - - ken. Seit
pp
pp
from that hour thine im - age fill'd My soul with light for
je - ner Stun - de verzehrt sich mein Leib, die See - - - le stirbt vor
Cres.
ev - - er; But ah! those tears I stole a - way, My heart from peace dis - sev - - er!
Seh - nen; mich hat das un - glück - sel - ge Weib ver - gift - et mit ih - ren Thrä - - nen.
pp
p
Decresc.

Neukomm.

Speed, my Bark! O, gent - ly speed thee, where - so - e'er the

Speed, my Bark! O, gent - ly speed thee, where - so - e'er the

soft tides lead thee! O'er the silver stream careering Where the graceful Swan is veering, Speed, my

soft tides lead thee! O'er the silver stream, the silver stream careering, Speed, my

Bark! O, gent - - - ly speed thee, Where - - - so - e'er .... the soft tides lead thee!

Bark! O, gent - - - ly speed thee, Where - - - so - e'er .... the soft tides lead thee!

By the moonlight's gracious beaming, By the golden stars' bright

gleam-ing,   Speed, my   Bark! O,   gent - ly

O! 'tis sweet this course unaided, When the scorching day has faded! Speed, my   Bark!   O,   gent - ly

speed   thee, where - so - e'er the soft   tides   lead   thee! Speed,   my Bark! O,

speed   thee, where - so - e'er the soft   tides   lead   thee!   Speed my gent - - ly speed thee, where - - so - e'er . . the soft tides lead thee!

Bark! O, speed thee, where - so - e'er . . the soft tides lead thee!

Let the world its strife pur -

su - - - - ing, Some up - - raise and oth - ers ru - in! Nought to-night shall

Nought to-night shall

give me sor-row; Come re - pose un - til the mor - row! Earth with all ..... its cares .... and

give me sor-row; Come re - pose un - til the mor - row! Earth with all ..... its cares .... and

seem - ing, Dies a - way in fair - y dream - ing: O! that here my life devoting, I might rest, thus

seem - ing, Dies a - way in fair - y dream - ing:

lightly float................ing, lead ....thee!

lead ....thee!

AH! WHAT AVAILS MY BLOOMING.
(TAUSENDSCHÓN.)

Carl Eckert.

Allegretto con moto.

1. Up - on a bronklet's bor - der. So beau - ti - ful to view, A -
1. *As ei - nes Büch - leins Ran - de, gar lieb - lich an - zu - sehn, da*
2. There came a mer - ry hun - ter: "My fair one, greeted be. Say
2. *Da kam der jun - ge Jä - ger: Gott grüss dich, Tau - send - schön, sag*

mid a group of wil - lows A win - some flow'ret grew. And ga - zing on the wa - ters
stand in grü - en Wal - de ein Blün - lein Tau - send - schön. Und in der Quel - le Spie - gel
wilt thou pret - ty flow - 'ret, Oh wilt thou dwell with me?" It look'd on him in rap - tures:
an, du hol - des Knösp - chen, willst du nicht mit mir gehn? Da blickt und nickt es lei - se:

It said in sad - dest tone: Ah! what a - vails my bloom - ing, If 'tis for me a -
sah es be - trübt hin - ein: Was hilft mir all mein Blüh - en, blüh ich für mich al -
Yes, I will be thine own! For 'tis but with a true heart One does not feel a -
Dein ei - gen will ich sein! Ach! nur an treu - em Her - zen, da ist man nicht al -

lone, Ah! what a - vails ... my bloom - ing, If 'tis for me a - lone.
lein, was hilft mir all ..... mein Blüh - en, blüh ich für mich al - lein.
lone, For 'tis but with ... a true heart, One does not feel a - lone.
lein, ach! nur an treu - em Her - zen, da ist man nicht al - lein.

OUT OF THE DEPTHS OF SORROW.

by Heine. ("AUS MEINEN GROSSEN SCHMERZEN.") R. Franz.

Andante.

Out of the depths of sor - row Rise these, the songs I sing you, On
Aus meinen gro - ssen Schmer - zen Mach ich die klei - nen Lie - - - der, Die

wings flutt'ring light, will they bring you, The love from my heart they bor - - - - row. Soon
he - ben ihr klin-gend Ge - fie - der, Und flattern nach ih - rem Her - - zen. Sie

from you the lays re - turn - ing, Come weeping a - loud and com-plain - ing, Their grief past my res -
fun - den den Weg zur Trau - ten, Doch kom - men sie wie - der und kla - gen, Und kla - gen und wol - len nicht

- strain - ing; The se - cret they heard ne'er learn - - - ing.
sa - gen, Was sie im Her - zen schau - - - ten.

AVE MARIA.

R. Franz.

Andante con moto tranquillo.

mf

p legato.

Ped.

1. A - ve Ma - ri - a! Sea and air are still, The sweet bells sound from many a
1. A - ve Ma - ri - a! Meer und Him - mel ruh'n, Von al - len Thür - men hallt der

dis - tant tow'r, A - ve Ma - ri - a! Safe from world - ly ill, Thou dwellest where the ransomed
Glo - cken - ton; A - ve Ma - ri - a! Laust man ird - schen Thun, Zur Jungfrau be - tet, zu der

Ped.

reign in pow'r. There heaven - ly le - gions wait to do God's will, And
Jung - frau Sohn; Des Him - mels Schaa - ren sel - ber knie - en nun, Mit

1st time.

crown with prai - ses ev' - ry rap - tured hour. And down thro' evening clouds descends the
Li - lien stä - ben vor des Va - ters Thron, Und durch die Ro - sen - wol - ken weh'n die

Ped.

2.

Hour of sweet musing! Heart and soul repose,
And dream of joys to come, in tranquil bliss.
O Faith! the heav'n-born, up through sunset glow,
On prayer's white wings to fairer worlds than this,
There dost thou mount, while tears assuage our woes.
For sorrow's brief, but joys are numberless.

       Ave Maria, &c.

2.

O heil'ge Andacht, welche jedes Herz
Mit leisen Schauern wunderbar durchdringt.
O heil'ger Glaube,—der sich himmelwärts
Auf des Gebetes weissem Fittig schwingt :
In milde Thränen löst sich da der Schmerz.
Indess der Freude Jubel sanfter klingt.—

       Ave Maria! &c.

WHEN THE QUIET MOON IS BEAMING.

(WENN SO SANFT UND MILD SELENE.)

J. Schondorf.

Moderato.

1. When the qui - - - et moon is beam - ing..... O - ver stream - let, vale and
1. *Wenn so sanft.......... und mild se - le - ne.....* *ü - ber Flur und wie - - sen*
2. strings..... my tears are fall - ing..... Ah! be - lov'd, what-e'er I
2. *Mond.......... ins Thal her - nie - der,..... hüllt in Nacht sich die Na -*

hill...... When the wea - - ry world lies dreaming All a - round, so calm and still; Then my
ruht,...... und in heil - ger, still - er Schöne zilbern fürlt die hei - - le Fluth Dann ach
seo...... All my van - ish'd bliss re - call - ing, Speaks of thee, of on - ly thee. Now thou'rt
tur...... denn er - klin - gen mei - ne Lie - der, su - chen dei - ne lie - - be Spur. Doch es

Ritenuto.

Poco Più Lento.

tune - ful lyre re - tak - ing. Oft I stray the woods a - mong, While my
fühl ich im - mer seh - nen in der schmerz be - weg - ten Brust,...... mei - ne
gone. my bu - ried treas - ure! Now the grass - green earth's thy tomb, Nought re -
bleibt mein heiss - es Seh - nen hin zu Dir, Ge - lieb - te mein,...... im - mer

Poco Più Lento.

heart its si - - lence breaking, Pours a flood of grief and song.
Lie - der lau - chen Thränen, nim - mer Froh - sinn nim - - mer Lust.
mains of joy and pleasure, All is sol - i - tude and gloom.
flies - sen mei - ne Thränen, nim - mer kann ich fröh - lich sein.

Ritard. *A Tempo.*

1st.
2. O'er the
2. Sinkt der
2nd.
Tempo 1mo.
3. Now the glo - - - rious sun...... ap - pear - - ing, All night's
3. Doch der - einst . . . . . wirst Du - - - - mir schei - - nen, strah - let
mf
shad - - ows flee...... a - way,.... Na - ture wak' - - - - - ning, warming,
hel - - - les Son - - - - - nen - licht, ... Und mein Herz . . . . hört auf zu
cheer - - ing. With the mag - - - - - - - ic of his ray.
wei - - nen, und mein herz . . . . ver - zwei - felt nicht.
Piu Lento.
Now Hope
Und ge -

whis - - pers, cease   to sor - row,   Soon shall cease thy grief, thy   pain,   Soon shall
stillt   ist dann   mein Seh - nen,   *nach dem   fer - - nen En - gels - - bild,*   *und ge -*

dawn   a bright - er mor - row,   When thou'lt meet   thy love   a - gain,   Soon shall
stillt   sind mei - - ne Thrä - nen,   *Du - - mein Herz bist en - - gel - mild,*   *und ge -*

dawn   a bright - er mor - row,   When thou'lt meet thy love   a - gain.
stillt   sind mei - - ne Thrä - nen;   Du - - mein Herz bist en - - gel - mild.

(GETRENTE LIEBE.)

L. Spohr.

Andante.

1. My dream of love is o - ver, I wake once more to
1. Der Lie - - be ban - gen Sor - gen, er bleicht der Freu - de
2. And now thou art an - oth - er's, Be hap - - py in thy
2. Du tönst der Schwermuth Lie - der, die sanft die Brust er -

pain. I've no one now to cheer me, But am a - lone - - a -
Strahl! Stets naht mir trüb der Mor - gen, und weckt der Schn - - sucht
choice. I nev - - er more shall see thee, Or bear thy thrill - - ing
- giesst. In stil - - ler an - dacht wie - der, das mild die Thrä - ne

gain; No joy can soothe my an - guish, Or heal my pangs so keen; Oh!
Qual; ich flieh die hei - tern Ta - ge und mei - ner Lie - be Kla - ge
voice. Yet from such thoughts and feel - ings, My heart I now must wean; Oh!
fliesst! O mög' der Tag nun schei - den, das ihr O mei - ne sai - ten, mit

would that we had nev - er met, Or part - ed ne'er had been.
sinkst du O stil - le Nacht wo nur der Kum - mer wacht!
would that we had nev - er met, Or part - ed ne'er had been.
mir die Nacht be - grüsst wo mild die Thrä - ne fliesst.

THE HERD-BELLS.

F. Gumbert.

Deep in the val - leys ring - ing, the herd bells e-cho clear; The

Deep in the val - leys ring - ing, the herd bells e-cho clear; The

wand'rer stops to list - - en, and fond - ly lin - gers here. The

wand'rer stops to list - - en, and fond - ly lin - gers here. The Kine bells tin-kle,

Kine bells tin - kle faint-ly, deep in the for - est grand, And in the ho - ly

faint - ly, deep in the for - est grand, So grand, and in the ho - ly twi - light make earth like spir - it land,   And in the ho - ly twi - light make

twi - light make earth like spir - it land,   And in the ho - ly twi - light make

Ritard.

earth like spir - it land.   2. Up -

Ritard.

earth like spir - it land.   2. Up

Ritard.

2nd verse.

Up - on the lof - ty mountains, they chime so sweet and   low, When tripp'd the high-est
                                                                 The wand'ring mu - sic

sum - mits, in ev' - ning's mel - low   glow; The wand'ring mu - sic   ren - ders   the
ren - ders   the   heart so warm. It   seems,

heart so warm. It seems   so   warm, ... a - mid sweet sounds to   en - ter the

land of heav'nly dreams, a - mid sweet sounds to en - ter the land of heav'nly dreams.

CRADLE SONG.

Composed by MENDELSSOHN

All.gretto non troppo.

1 Slum - - - ber! Slum- ber and dream in the
2 Slum - - - ber! Slum- ber and dream of the

morning of life, Dream of the pathway be - fore thee, Let not each hour with
fresh smil- ing spring, Bear- ing her man- tle of flow - ers, Night-in- gales woo thee

sor- row be rife . . . . Hap- pi - ness too ho- vers o'er thee, Happiness
Mis- tress and sing . . . Strains thro' the star spangled hours, Strains thro' the

too hovers o'er   thee,   Life thus is checker'd with sunshine and sorrow, Dark may the day be but brighter the
star spangled hours   Time with a   gentle wing, by thee is glancing, Spring like the morning of life is ad-

mor - row: Then never be impatient!   Then never be impatient!
- - van - cing: Then never be impatient!   &c.

ne - - - ver, then never be   im - pa - - - tient!

Slum - - - ber!

GREEN SHADES THAT I LOVE.

(WILLKOMMEN MEIN WALD.)

R. Franz.

Green shades that I love, where branch - es to me Rustle soft - ly a
Will - kom - men mein Wald, grün - schat - ti - ges Haus ! Durch die Wi - pfel schon

wel - come, Where light bree - zes free, Roam fra - graut, a - round me, no
hüllt mir dein grü - ssend Ge - braus. Wie trink' ich in Zü - gen mich

cares an - noy, And here I breathe free - ly with heart - felt
frisch und ge - sund, Hier athm' ich Ge - nü - gen aus Her - - zens

joy, with heart - - - - felt joy. . . . . . .
grund, aus Her - - - zens - grund . . . . . .

From ver — dant hill-side, and fair valleys wide, Comes the mu - si-cal
Zum an — si-gen Hang, auf-stei — gend vom Thal,.... Dringt der Ho — - - ckrn

clang of the eve — ning bells. And the sun - set's red glow, these old
Klang und des A — bends Strahl. Und es rauscht in der Ei — che hoch

branch - es be - low. Lights far to the depths of the fern — clad
stre — ben - dem Baum, Im grü — nen Be - rei — che ein Lie — des

dells, the fern — clad dells.
traum, ein Lie — — des - traum.

Sweet flow - 'rets a - dorn the scene a - round, I look on the
Den Blu - men ge - sellt auf Ra - sen und Moos. Tief schau' ich die

skies with their blue pro - found. And I dream, as the sha - dows lull
Weh und den Him - mel wie gross! Und ich träu - me im Schwei - gen der

soft, soft to rest That I am of all this fair earth pos -
schat - ti - gen Ruh' Den Him - mel mein ei - gen, die Er - de da

- sessed, of air and earth pos - sess'd.
- zu, die Er - de da - zu!

BARCAROLE.

F. Kucken.

Bounding, bounding boat go light - ly O'er the swelling wa - ter,

Bounding, bounding boat go light - ly O'er the swelling wa - ter,

O! . . . Tilting, tilt-ing wave gleam brightly, In the starlight's golden glow!

O! . . . Tilting, tilt-ing waves gleam brightly, In the starlight's golden glow! Thro' the

Thro' the still night sound, O Song, Where love lingers list'ning long, Where love

still night sound, O Song, Where love ling - ers list'ning long, Thro' the still night sound, O

Dim.
p
ling - ers, where love ling - ers, ling-ers list'-ning long; Bound - ing, bounding, bounding boat go light - ly,
p
song where love ling - ers, ling-ers list'-ning long; Bound - ing, bounding, bounding boat go light - ly
sf p
sf p
O'er the swell - ing wa - ter O!.... Tilting, tilting wave, gleam brightly In the starlight's gold - en
O'er the swell - ing wa - ter O!.... Tilting, tilting wave, gleam brightly In the starlight's gold - en
dol.
glow! Thro' the still night sound, O Song! Where . . love ling-ers list'ning long, Where love
molto espress.
dol.
glow! Thro' . . . the still night sound. O Song!
p

ling - - - ers, list'ning long,   Where love ling - - ers, list'ning long . . .   Lo I my

love there on the beach is,   Play-ful ran . . . she on be-fore !   Lo I her longing, faithful arms she

reach - es   Forth to greet . . me from the shore,   Yes, my true love,   on the beach is,   playful

Lo ! my love, there on the beach is.   Play-ful, playful, play-ful

p f
ran she on be-fore! Lo! her faith-ful arms she reaches, Forth to greet me from the
p mfz p f p
ran she on before! Lo! her longing, faithful arms she reaches, Forth to greet me from the
p sf
sf Ritard. tempo.
shore, Bound - ing, bounding, bounding boat go lightly, O'er the swelling wa-ter O!
shore, Bound - ing, bounding, bounding boat go lightly, O'er the swelling wa-ter O!
Ritard. tempo.
f p
Tilting, tilting wave, gleam light-ly In the star-light's gold - en glow! Thro' . . the still night,
Tilting, tilting wave, gleam lightly In the star-light's gold - - en glow! Thro' the still night sound, O Song! Thro' .... the

sound, O Song! where love ling - ers, where love ling - ers list'ning

still night sound, O Song! Where love ling - ers list'ning long, where love ling - ers list'ning

long. still night sound, O Song! . . . . where love ling - ers.

long. Thro' the still night sound, O Song! where love ling - - ers. Thro' the

Still . . . . still night . . . .

still night sound, O Song, Where love ling - - - - - - ers. Still . . . . . . still night . . . .

NINETTA.

(VENETIANISCHES GONDELLIED.)

G. Stigelli.

Allegretto Moderato.

1. When through the Pia - zet - - ta The ev' - - ning airs sigh; Then know'st thou, Ni -
1. Wenn durch die Pia - zet - - ta die A - - bend - luft weht; Dann weisst du, Ni -
2. Mean - while, in a Mar - i - ner's garb I ap - pear; And tremb - ling - ly
2. Ein Schif - - fer - kleid trag ich zur sel - - - - bi - gen Zeit, Und zit - - ternd dann

- net - ta, Who waits for thee nigh; When through the Pia - zet - - ta The ev' - ning airs
- net - ta, wer war - tend hier steht. Wenn durch die Pia - zet - - ta - - e A - - bend - luft
whis - per, the boat's read - y near. Mean - while in a Mar - iner's garb I ap -
sag ich: dass Boot ist be - - reit. Ein Schif - - fer - kleid trag ich zu sel - - - bi - gen

sigh, Then know'st thou, Ni - net - ta, Who waits for thee nigh. La la...... la la la
weht, Dann weisst du, Ni - net - ta, wer war - tend hier steht. La la...... la la la
pear, And tremb - ling - ly whis - per, The boat's read - y near. La la...... la la la
Zeit Und zit - - ternd dann sag ich, das Boot ist be - - reit. La la...... la la la

Dolce.

la la la la la...... la la...... la la...... la la la la la la....
la la la la la...... la la...... la la...... la la la la la la.

Des - pite   of the   mask   and the   veil   I may   wear.   Thou'lt know,   my Ni -
Du   weisst   wer trotz   Mas - ke und   Schlei - er dich   kennt   Du   weisst   wie die
O   come   now, see   Lu - na 'mid   clouds   flit - ting   by!   So   thro'   the La -
O   komm   jetzt wo   Lu - nen noch   Wol - ken durch   zieh'n,   lass   durch   die La -

- net - ta, who waits   for thee   there.   La.....   la la   la....   la la   la....   la la
Sehn - sucht im   Her - zen mir   brennt.   La.....   la la   la..   la la   la....   la la
- gu - na, Be - lov'd, let us   fly.   La.....   la la   la   la la   la   la la
- gu - nen, Ge - lieb - te, uns   flien.   La   la la   la   la la   la   la la

la....   la....   la la   la....   la la   la....   la la   la....
la   la   la la   la   la la   la   la la   la

Yes,................   Thou'lt know,   my Ni - net - ta, Who waits   for   thee
Ja................   Du   weisst   wie die Sehn - sucht im   Her - zen   mir
Yes,................   So thro'   the La - gu - na, Be - lov'd,   let   us
Ja................   Lass durch   die La - gu - nen, Ge - lieb - te,   uns

there.................. Thou'lt know, my Ni - net - ta, Who waits for thee there. La
brennt.................. Du weisst wie die Sehn - sucht im Her - zen mir brennt. La
fly.................. So thro' the La - gu - na, Be - lov'd, let us fly. La
flieh'n.................. Lass durch die La - gu - nen, Ge - lieb - te, uns flieh'n. La
Dolce.
la...... la la...... la la la la la la...... Thou'lt know, my Ni - net - ta, Who
la la la la la la la la la. Du weisst wie die Sehn - sucht im
la...... la la...... la la la la la la...... So thro' the La - gu - na, Be -
la la la la la la la la la. Lass durch die La - gu - nen, Ge -
waits for thee there. La la...... la la...... la la la la la la...... Thou'lt
Her - zen mir brennt. La la la la la la la la la la Du
lov'd, let us fly. La la...... la la...... la la la la la la...... So,
- lieb - te, uns flieh'n. La la la la la la la la la la Lass
know, my Ni - net - ta, Who waits for......... thee there.
weisst wie die Sehn - sucht im Her - - - zen......... mir brennt.
So thro' the La - gu - na, Be - lov'd, let......... us fly.
durch die La - gu - - nen, Ge - lieb - - - te......... uns flieh'n

LONGING.

(SEHNSUCHT.)

R. F. Hunt.

1. So far a - way, so far a - way, Thou canst not hear my songs of
1. Du Bist so weit von mir, so weit, Du hörst nicht mein - - er Sehnsucht
2. The moon looks on the lone - ly way Where erst we sought her light to -
2. Der Mond er sah uns sanft ver - eint, Blickt still und trau - - rig auf mich

sad - ness O end this end - less part - ing day, Come back my love, come back my glad...
Lie - der, es giebt kein Leid - wie Trennungs - leid, Komm wie - der, O mein Lieb komm wie...
- geth - er; The clouds have wept with me to - day. And thou, my love! O has - ten hith
nie - der, Die wolke hat mit mir ge - weint, Und du, mein Lieb! Mein Lieb, komm wie -

ness.
der.
er!
der!

Poco rallent.   *A Tempo.*

COME TO ME DEAREST MAIDEN!

Words by Heme. (KOMM!) G. Meyerbeer.

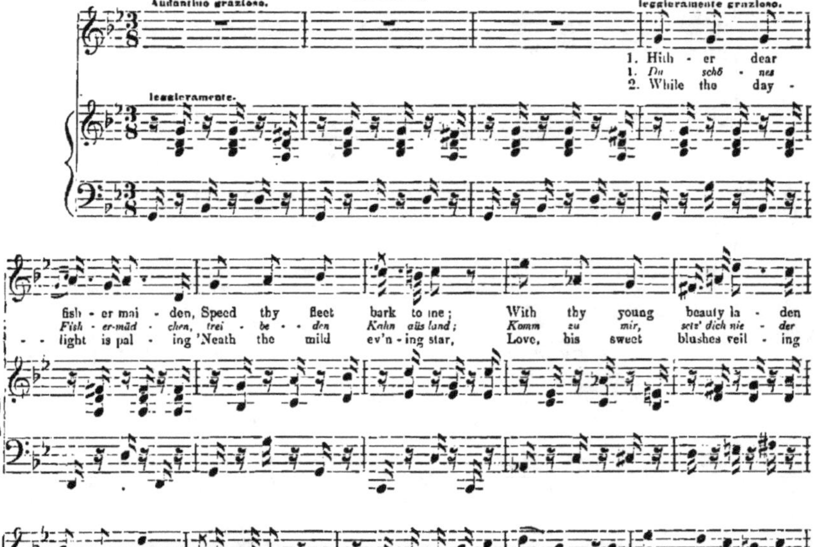

E'en as that rest - less o - cean, Throbs this wild heart of mine,
Mein herz gleicht ganz dem Meere, hat Sturm und Eb' und Fluth,
Toss'd on doubt's sur - ges lone - ly, Let me thy pi - ty move.

But 'neath its dark commo - tion, Love's pre - cious pearl is thine, Come!
Und man - che schöne Per - le In si - ne tie - fe ruht, Komm!
Wreck not the hope whose on - ly Suc - cor can be thy love, Come!

Come! For thee I pine, dear mai - den, Come! Come! Oh bring thy heart to
Komm! da schönes Fis - her - müd - chen, Komm! Komm! wir kom en hand in

mine! Come! Come! Come!
hand, Komm! Komm! Komm!

IRENE.

Franz Abt.

1. Whether I love thee? ask but the star-lets, To whom I've
1. Ob ich dich lie - be? fra - ge die Ster - ne de - nen ich

oft - en in ag - o - ny sued.   Wheth - er I love thee? ask but this rose-bud, Which I now
oft mei - ne Kla - gen ver - traut.   Ob ich dich lie - be? fra - ge die Ro - se, die ich dir

send thee, with warm tears be - dewed.   Whether I love thee? ask but this rose-bud, Which I now
sen - de, von Thrä - nen be - thaut.   Ob ich dich lie - be? fra - ge die Ro - se, die ich dir

send thee, with warm tears be - dewed.
sen - de von Thrä - nen be - thaut.

2. Wheth - er I love thee? ask but the light clouds, Which have so
2. Ob ich dich lie - be? fra - ge die Wol - ken, de - nen ich
3. Did'st thou but love me, heav - en - ly maid - en, Oh then I'd
3. Wenn du mich lieb - test, himm - lisch - es Mäd - chen, O dann ye

oft - en my sor - rows con - veyed, Wheth - er I love thee? ask but the streamlets, In each I've
oft mei - ne Bot - schaft er traut. Ob ich dich lie - be? fra - ge die Wel - len, ich hab in
own to thee, own it with pride, That I do love thee, that I do call thee Al - ways my
stän - de ich dir es auch laut, Wie ich dich lie - be, das ich dich nen - ne stets meinen

Poco Stringendo.   *A Tempo.*

oft - en thy im - age sur - veyed. Whether I love thee? ask but the streamlets, In each I've
je - der dein Bild - niss ge - schaut. Ob ich dich lie - be? fra - ge die Wel - len, ich hab in
un - gel, and soon, my bride. That I do love thee, that I do call thee Al - ways my
En - gel, und bald mei - ne Braut. Wie ich dich lie - be, das ich dich nen - ne stets mei - nen

Poco Stringendo.   *A tempo.*

Dim.

oft - en thy im - age sur - veyed.
je - der dein bild - niss ge - schaut.
an - gel, and soon, my bride.
Eng - el, und bald mei - ne Braut.

Dim.   *Fine.*

GOOD NIGHT, FAREWELL.

(GUT' NACHT, FAHR' WOHL.)

Fr. Kücken.

1. Good night, fare - well, my own true heart, A thou - sand
1. Gut' Nacht, fahr' wohl, mein treu - es Herz, zu tau - send
2. I see thy heart re - flect - ed, by A star with
2. Ich seh' Dein gan - zes Herz im Blick, wie Him - mel

times good night.......... Each thought of thee bids grief de -
gu - te Nacht, wie hab' ich einst in Wonn' und
in the stream.......... It shines forth from thy clear blue
in der Fluth, gut' Nacht, fahr' wohl', Du all' mein

part, And ren - ders joy more bright. Tho' far, tho'
Schmerz, herz - in - nig Dein ge - dacht! Bist fern, doch
eye, And sheds o'er me its beam. And tho' no
Glück, mein Herz an Dei - nem ruht! Sonst hab' ich

Sempre Cres.
im - age dwells with me, Thou art my guid - - - ing
bleibt dein Bild mein Traum, mein Stern in dunk - - - ler
more than one bright glance I e'er of thee pos -
nichts, ach nichts von Dir, als die - - sen Blick al - -
Cres. Ped. mf Ped. Ped. Sempre Cres.
Cres.
star. When o'er me dark - - - ning clouds I
Nacht, der glän - - zt hell am Wol - - - ken -
- sess'd That look my heart will e'er en -
- lein, und wei - - chest e - - - wig Du von
Marcato. Ped. f Ped. ff Ped. Ped. Ped.
see, Thy love guides me a - - far, When
saum, wo Leid und Lie - - be wacht, der
- trance, and ren - - der ev - - er blest That
mir, Dein Blick bleibt e - - - wig mein, und
p Ped. f

o'er me dark - - - ning clouds I see, Thy love guides
glan - - zet hell am Wol - - - ken - - saum, wo Leid und
look my heart will o'er en - - trance, And ren - - der
wei - - - chest e - - - - - uig Du von mir, Dein Blick bleibt
Rit.
Ped.
p
me a - - far. Fare - well........... my own true
Lie - - be wacht! Fahr' wohl, mein treu - - es
ev - - er blest.
e - - - wig mein.
Cres - cen - - - do.
pp
stac.
heart, A thou - sand times fare - well! Good night, fare - well, my
Herz, zu tau - - send gu - - te Nacht, gut' Nacht, fahr' wohl, mein
Cres.
Rit.
Dim.
Tranquillo.
Dol.
ff
own true heart...............
treu - - es Herz...............
Andante.
Sostenuto.
Marcato.

Franz Abt

1. When the swal-lows homeward fly, When the ros - es scatter'd lie, When from nei - ther hill nor dale, Chants the
2. When the white swan southward roves, To seek at noon the orange groves, When the red tints of the west, Prove the
3. Hush! my heart, why thus complain? Thou must too thy woes con-tain; Though on earth no more we rove, Fond - ly

pp stringendo. Ritard.

sil - very night - in - gale; In these words my bleed-ing heart, Would to thee its grief im-
sun has gone to rest; In these words my bleeding heart, Would to thee its grief im-
breath-ing vows of love; Thou, my heart, must find re - lief, Yield-ing to these words be-

pp Stringendo colla parte.

Ten. A Tempo.

tart, When I thus thy im - age lose, Can I, ah!
part, When I thus thy im - age lose, Can I, ah!
lief; I shall see thy form a - gain, Though to

can I e'er know re - pose, Can...... I, ah! can I e'er know re - pose.
can I e'er know re - pose? Can...... I, ah! can I e'er know re - pose?
day we part a - gain, Though.. to - day we part a - gain.

sf

HOME.

Music by A. ABT.

Moderato con espressione.

1. Guardian moth-er! Pa-rent land! Nurse of all our kindred band!
1. Mut-ter-er - de, hei-lig land! wo-der Freu-den Wie-ge stand!

1. Guardian moth-er! Pa-rent land! Nurse of all our kindred band!

Still of treasured thoughts the near-est, Ev-er honored, ev-er dear-est,
Dei-ner denk' ich nah' und fer-ne, theure Heimath e-wig ger-ne,

Still of treasured thoughts the near-est, Ev-er honored, ev-er dear-est,

Where I first (O sacred earth!) Looked on her who gave me birth,
wo zu-erst ich froh beglückt nach der Mut-ter hin-ge-blickt!

Where I first (O sacred earth!) Looked on her who gave me birth,

HOME. Concluded.

2

Home of all my best beloved!
Where, untouched by care, I roved;
Where, 'mid smiles and play, seemed given
To my heart a daily heaven.
How, ah! how, methinks I see
Childhood's day again with thee;
Where, untouched by care, I roved,
Home of all my best beloved!

3

Guardian Mother! Eden blest!
Holy shelter! lap of rest!
Long as aught of life I cherish,
Till its last fond pulses perish,
Joys that all to thee belong
Still shall be my duteous song
Nurse of all our kindred band!
Guardian Mother! Parent land

2

Heimath, Heimath, lieb und traut!
Wo ich einst mir aufgebaut
Unter Lust und Spiel und Scherzen
Einen Himmel meinem Herzen.
Taglich schau' ich gern zuruck
Nach der Kindheit reichem Gluck!
Heimath, Heimath, lieb und traut!
Theure Heimath lieb und traut!

3

Muttererde, Paradies!
Welch' ein Laut so lieb und sus_!
Will, so lang mir Blumen bluhen,
Rosig meine Wangen gluhen,
Singen oft aus froher Brust,
Freuen mich der Heimath Lust!
Muttererde, Paradies!
Welch ein Laut so lieb und sus

EVENING.

(ABENDS.)

Words by J. Von Eichendorf.

R. Franz.

Andantino.

Evening sounds fill all the wood, Bird and in-sect sing - ing, Soon will kin - dle plan-et, star;
A - bend - lich schon rauscht der Wald, Aus den tief - sten Grün - den, Dro - ben wird der Herr nun bald,

'Mid them angel's wing - ing, Gaze down in the dusk profound, List each tranquil evening sound.
Bald die Stern an-zün - den; Wie so still - e in den Grün-den A - bend-lich nur rauscht der Wald.

All re - tire to tran-quil rest, Save the wand'rer roaming. Hears the moan of wood and sea,
Al - les geht zu sei - ner Ruh', Wald und Welt ver-sau - sen, Schauernd hört der Wand-rer zu,

Hastens thro' the gloaming. Here, my heart, by sweet tho'ts blest. Sink in for-est shades to rest.
Senkt sich wohl noch Hau - se; Hier in Wal - des grü - ner Klause, Herz, geh' end - lich du auch zur Ruh'.

MAIDENS' EYES THEIR HEARTS REVEAL.

Composed by GUMBERT.

1. Maid-ens' eyes their hearts re - veal, Those bright orbs read oft, fond lov - - er,
2. Oh! 'tis beau - - ti - ful to see Fond eyes one an - oth - er read - - ing,

If their charms you would dis - cov - er, If Love's se - - - cret you would steal,
Looks of love with love - looks plead - ing, Nev - er words could speak like these,

What the eye de - clares re - ceive, Try and trust its full ex - pres - - - - sion,
Flash - ing sun-beams may des - cry Beau - teous hues in dia - mond fa - - - - ces,

MAIDENS' EYES THEIR HEARTS REVEAL. Concluded.

But your fair ones' word con - fes - - - sions, Friend, be - ware how to be - lieve! Friend, be -

Rich - er soul - hues, true heart - gra - - - ces, Own the witch - ing of the eye, Own the

ware how to be - lieve. Maid-ens' eyes their hearts re - veal, Those bright

witch - - ing of the eye.

orbs read oft, fond lov - - - er, Maidens' eyes their hearts re - veal, Maid-ens' eyes their hearts re-

veal, Those bright orbs, those bright orbs...... read oft, fond lov - - - er.

Composed by KÜCKEN.

1 My harp now lies brok - en, its mu - sic has fled, My
2 O where are the sons of the ra - ces of old, In
3 The hea - vy chains rat - tle that fet - ter the arms Of

heart like its strains in my bo - som lies dead; The anxious bird
bat - tle they've fall - en and lie stiff and cold; The town smokes in
Ju - dah's fair daughters, once famed for their charms, The days pass on

THE MAID OF JUDAH. Continued.

flut - ters   by toils   when be - set,   And   dies   while its   strug - gling   when
ru - ins   the vale is   laid   waste.   The   blood   of the   slain   has   its
slow - ly   and drea - ry   the   nights,   While   still   in our   bon - dage   the

caught in   the net.   Oh!   land   of my   fathers   Oh!   land   dear to
ver - dure   de - faced.   Oh!   land   of my   fathers   Oh!   land   dear to
fue - nun   de - light.   Oh!   land   of my   fathers   Oh!   laud   dear to

me,   Thou   ne - ver   a   gain shalt my   rest - ing   place   be;   Oh!
me,   Say   when will   Je - ho - vah   our   veng - ing   God   be;   Oh!
me,   Might I   in   death be   u - ni - ted   to   thee!   Oh!

THE MAID OF JUDAH. Concluded.

land of my fa - thers, oh! land dear to me, . . .
land of my fa - thers, oh! land dear to me, ...
land of my fa - thers, oh! land dear to me . . . .

Ne - ver more shalt thou my rest - - - - - - - ing place
When will Je - ho - vah, our veng - - - - - - - ing God
Might I in death be u - ni - - - - - - - - ted to

be.
be.
thee.

THE EXILE.

(LAND MEINER SEELIGSTEN.)

C. Keller

Adagio expressivo.

1. Swift fades the land I love bo
1. *Land mei - ner see - ligs - ten Ge*

- hind   me, The   ra - ging sea be - fore me   lies,   The   drea - ry wind so cold - ly
füh - - - le, von rein - sten Mor-gen-thau be - straut, um säu - selt von der Him - mel's

blow - ing But ech - o's back my mourn - ful sighs.   May   heav'n watch
Küh - - le, und von der Fan - ta - sie ge - - weiht.   Land   mei - ner

o'er thee, while far,   while   far from thee I   roam,   Fare - well, thou land where hope is
Ju - gend, ach ver - schlos - sen auf e - wig bist du mir!   so   schnell ist mir dein Glück ver -

2.

Where-e'er my cruel fate shall guide me,
My heart for thee shall ever burn,
In mem'ry though I oft may see thee,
Alas! for me there's no return.
  May heav'n watch, &c.

2.

Durchzog ich auch die ganze Erde,
Mein Herz blieb stets bei dir zurück,
Wo ich auch bin und noch seyn werde,
Schwebst du vor meinen Thränenblick.
  Land meiner, &c

THE MILLER'S FLOWERS.

(DES MÜLLERS BLUMEN.)

F. Schubert.

1. So ma - ny flow'rs of a - zure hue, do near a flow - ing stream - let grow, The
1. Am Bach viel klei - ne Blu - men steh'n, aus hel - len blau - en Au - gen seh'n, der
2. Be - neath her lit - tle win - dow seat, there I will plant these flow - ers sweet, When

stream - let is a friend of mine, and sky - blue dar - ling's eyes do shine.
Bach, der ist des Mül - lers Freund, und hell - blau Lieb - chen's Au - ge scheint,
all's at rest, oh, then re - mind, and when her head's to sleep inclined,
ruft ihr zu wenn Al - les schweigt, wenn sich ihr Haupt zum Schlummer neigt!

Dim.

Hence those I call my flow - ers, hence those I call my flow -
d'rum sind es mei - ne Blu - men, d'rum sind es mei - ne Blu -
Ye know what - e'er I mean, ye know what - e'er I
ihr wisst ja was ich mei - ne, ihr wisst ja was ich mei -

pp

Cres.

- ers.
- men.
mean.
ne.

Above the Stars there is Rest.

(UEBER DEN STERNEN IST RUH)

FRANZ ABT.

Andante.

1. A - bove the stars, there is rest! A-
1. Ue - ber den Ster - nen ist Ruh!..........
2. A - bove the stars, there is rest! A-
2. Ue - ber den Ster - nen ist Ruh!..........

bove the stars, there is rest! Suf-fer, in pa-tience con-fi - - - ding,
Ue - ber den Ster-nen ist Ruh! Dul - de, o dul - de hie - nie - - - den,
bove the stars, there is rest! Bear up, to life's ills re-sign - - ing,
Ue - ber den Ster-nen ist Ruh! Dul - de, o dul - de auf's Neu - - - - e,

Life, with its tri - al and chid - - - ing; There, peace e - ter - nal, a - bid - - -
Wenn dir zu lei - den be - schie - - - den, Dor - ten in e - wi-gem Frie - - -
There, where the sun is still shin - - ing, Comes nei-ther grief nor re - pin - -
Dor - ten, in e - wi-ger Bläu - - - e, Woh - net nicht Kum - mer, nicht Reu - -

ing, Makes the de - light of the blest. . . . . Dark, tho' to - day be with
den La - chet nur Won - ne dir zu. . . . . Was dich hie - nie - den ge -
ing; There are re - liev'd the op - prest. . . . . On-ward, with courage re -
e, Dor - ten ge - ne - sest auch du!. . . . . Was dir die Wun - den ge -

sor - - - row, Hope gilds more bright - ly the mor - - - row;
trof - - - fen, O welch ein se - li - ges Hof - - - fen:
viv - - - ing, Ev - er still pa - tient - ly striv - - - ing,
schla - - - gen, Musst es ge - dul - dig er - tra - - - gen:

f *pp ritard.*

O'er yon fair stars there is rest! . . . O'er the fair
Ue - ber den Ster - nen ist Ruh!. . . . . Ue - ber den

f *pp* *rit.* *p*

stars there is rest! . . .
Ster - nen ist Ruh!. . . . .

When I know that Thou art near Me.

(WEISS ICH DICH IN MEINER NÄHE.)

F. ABT.

Con espressione.

When I
Weiss ich

know that thou art near me, In my heart are joy and rest; I to slum-ber, soft con-
Dich in mei-ner Nä-he, hab' ich Frie-den hab' ich Ruh,' schliesse, wenn ich schlafen

fide me,— Close my eyes, su-preme-ly blest. Close my eyes, su -
ge - he, still - be - glückt die Au - gen zu, still - be-glückt die

Close my eyes, ... su -
still - be - glückt.... die

preme-ly blest.
Au - gen zu.

From thee
Ach, und

preme-ly blest. Where an an - gel guards the dwell - ing, There is joy and bliss di - vine.
Au - gen zu. Wo ein gu - - ter En-gel wei - - let, ist der Frie - de rings um - her;

part - ed, past all tell - ing, is the an - guish that is mine.
bist du fort-ge - ei - - let, hab'ich kein - nen Frie-den mehr.

poco accelerando.

Where an an - gel guards the
Wo ein gu - - ter En-gel

From thee part - ed, past all tell - ing, Is the
Ach, und bist du fort-ge - ei - let, hab'ich

dwell - ing, There is joy and bliss di - vine.
wei - let, ist der Him - - mel rings um - her,

There is joy and bliss, is
ist der Him - mel, ist der

ritard. *a tempo.* pp

sor - row that is mine. When I know that thou art near me, In my heart are joy and rest.
kei - nen Frieden mehr. Weiss ich Dich in meiner Nä - he, hab' ich Frieden, hab' ich Ruh'.

ritard. *a tempo.*
pp

joy and bliss di - vine. When I know that thou art near me, In my heart are joy and rest. I to
Him - mel rings um - her. Weiss ich Dich in meiner Nä - he, hab' ich Frieden, hab' ich Ruh'. Schliesse,

pp

I to slumber soft con - fide me. Close my eyes, su-preme-ly blest, Close my
schliesse, wenn ich schlafen ge - he. still - be - glückt die Au - gen zu, still - be -

pp
p

slumber soft con - fide me. Close my eyes, su-preme-ly blest, Close my
wenn ich schla - fen ge - he. still - be - glückt die Au - gen zu, still - be -

pp poco riten.

eyes, su - preme-ly blest. When I know that thou art near me!
glückt die Au - gen zu. Weiss ich Dich in meiner Nä - he!

pp

eyes, su - preme-ly blest. When I know that thou art near me!
glückt die Au - gen zu. Weiss ich Dich in meiner Nä - he!

pp pp

Dear Angel, Sleep thee Well.

(SCHLAF WOHL, DU SÜSSER ENGEL DU.)

FRANZ ABT.

Moderato.

1. O gen - tle night! O gen - tle night! The world is hush'd, the stars are
1. Rings stil - le herscht es schweight der Wald, voll - en - det ist des Ta - ges

2. Ah! hast thou thought of me to - day! I think of thee, for thee I
2. Ob du auch heut an mich ge - dacht! Ich dacht an dich wohl für und

bright, And birds have long since ceas'd to sing, And slumber soft, with folded wing. Sleep
Lauf der Vöglein Lied ist längst ver-hallt am Him-mel ziehn die Ster - ne auf. Schlafe

pray, And nightly cry, thy lattice near, "Good-night, sweet angel, ever dear!"
für und ru - fe jetzt dir "gu - te Nacht" ver - bor-gen still vor dei - ner Thür.

marc.

cresc.

molto espressivo.

soft, sleep well, . . . And let thy wea - ry eye - lids close; sleep
wohl schlafe wohl . . . . . und schliess die schö - nen Au - gen zu, schlafe

soft, sleep well, sweet an - gel, yield thee to re - pose!
wohl schlafe wohl du sü - sser lie - ber En - gel du!

Ah! 𝄏
Ob

3. In dreams, thy sis - ter an-gels come. From out their dis - tant heav'nly
3. Es schwe - - be aus des Him-mels Raum ein heil' - ger Bo - te dir zur

sempre pp

home; Thy vis - ions fill with heav'nly peace, And bid thy rap-ture still in
Nacht und brin - ge dir den schön-sten Traum, bis du zum Morgen neu er -

pp

crease. Sleep soft, sleep well, and let thy weary eye-lids
wacht. Schlafe wohl, schla-fe wohl, und schliess die schönen Au-gen

close; sleep soft, sleep well, und an-gels guard
zu, schla-fe wohl, schla-fe wohl, du sü-sser lie-

thy sweet re-pose; sleep soft, may
ber En-gel du! Schlaf wohl du

an-gels watch thy sweet re-pose.
lie-ber sü-sser En-gel du!

Thousand Greetings.

(TAUSEND GRUESSE.)

F. ABT.

Moderato.

p   *cres.*   *p*   *p*

p legg. e grazioso.

Should a zeph - yr on thy cheek leave a kiss, re - treat - ing, Think, my dear, 'tis
Küss - et dir ein Lüftchen fein Wan - gen o - der Hän - de, den - ke dass es

p.   *p*   *pp*

pochett. ritard.   *pp*   *mf*

I who seek So to send thee greet - ing. Thou - - sands have I
Grü - sse sein, dir ich zu dir sen - de. Tau - - send send ich

legato.   *cres.*

sent thee so, Round thy house to whisper low: O that I were near thee!
täg-lich aus, dass sie we-hen um dein Haus, wie ich dein ge-den-ke,
O that I were near thee! Thou-sands send I eve-ry day....... thousands thou-sands eve-ry
wie ich dein ge-den-ke, tau-send send ich täg-lich aus, ... tau-send, tau-send send ich
day.
aus.
animato.
cres.
legg. e grazioso.
If to thee a lit-tle bird Should come fly-ing o-ver, Think it is to
Komm' ein klei-nes Vö-ge-lein zu dir hin-ge-flo-gen, denk es sei die
dim.
pp
p
f

pochett. ritard.
pp
mf
bring thee word, From thy lone-some lov - er. Hear what he would
Sehnsucht mein, die dir nach ge - zo - - gen. Hö - - re was sie
legato. cres.
fond-ly say: Think of me so far a - way, O that I were near thee!
freundlich spricht, und ver - giss des Fer-nen nicht, der nur dein ge - den - ket,
p
f
pp
dim.
O that I were near thee! Hear the pret-ty war - bler say: Think of me so far a-
der nur dein ge - den - - ket hö - re was sie freun-dlich spricht, und ver - giss des Fer - nen
way.
nicht.
animato.
cres.

Dedication.

(WIDMUNG.)

R. SCHUMANN.

Thou art my soul, thou art my heart; Thou both my
Du meine See - le, du mein Herz, du meine

joy and sadness art; Thou art my world, where I am mov - er, My heav'n art
Wonn' O du mein Schmerz, Du meine Welt, in der ich le - be, mein Him - mel

thou where - in I hov - er; Thou art my grave, where - in I
Du, du rein ich schwe - - be, O du mein Grab, in das hin -

cast for ev - - - er all my sor - - - row past!
ab ich e - - - - wig mei - nen Kum - - - mer gab!

ritard.

thou art my rest, my peace .... pro - tect - ing,
du bist die Ruh', du bist .... der Frie - - den,

Thou art from Heav'n my life .... di - rect - ing; Make me, by
du bist vom Him - - - - - mel mir. .... be - schie - den Dass du mich

worth, thy love to own! Thy glance to me myself hath shown! Thou'rt ev - er
liebst, macht mich mir werth, dein Blick hat mich vor mir ver - klärt, du liebst mich

ritard.

round me hov - 'ring by, My guar - dian sprite, my bet - ter
lie - - - - - bend ü - ber mich, mein gu - - ter Geist, mein bess - 'res

ritar - dan - do.

I! / Ich! Thou art my soul, thou art my heart; / Du meine Seele, du mein Herz, Thou both, my / du meine

joy, / Wonn' and sadness art; / O du mein Schmerz, Thou art my world, / du meine Welt, where I am mov-er, / in der ich le--be, My heav'n art / mein Him-mel

thou, / du, where-in I hov--er, / darein ich schwe--be, my guardian spirit, / mein gu-ter Geist, my bet--ter I! / mein bess-'res Ich!

The Slumber-Song.

(SCHLUMMERLIED.)

"GENTLY REST."

Composed by F. KÜCKEN

Moderato. con espressione.

1. All is still in sweet — est rest, Be thy
1. Al — — les still in süs — — ser Ruh, d'rum mein
2. Gent — — ly rest! the night stars gleam, Soft thy

sleep se — rene — ly blest! Winds are moan — ing
Kind so schlaf auch du! draus — — sen säu — — selt
slum — ber; bright thy dream. Fear no harm, for

o'er the wild, Lul — — la — by, sleep on.... my
nur der Wind, Su, su, au! schlaf ein.... mein
I will keep Watch with love, while thou'rt a —

Sf

Ped. ♭♭ · * ♭ ·

2 Close each little peepsy eye,
Let them like two roselets lie;
And when purpling morn shall glow,
Still as roselets freshly blow,
Still as roselets freshly blow;
La, lullaby, sleep on, my child,
May angel gleams
Pervade thy dreams!

4 While those buds the mother tends,
And with kisses o'er them bends,
She ne'er heeds the spring-tide near;
Spring and summer wait her here;
Spring and summer wait her here,
La, lullaby, sleep on, my child.
May angel gleams
Pervade thy dreams!

3 Schliesse deine Augelein,
Lass sie wie zwei Knospen sein!
Morgen wenn die Sonn' erglüht,
Sind sie wie die Blum' erblüht,
Sind sie wie die Blum' erblüht,
Su, su, su, su! schlaf ein mein Kind.
Su, su, su, su!
In guter Ruh'!

4 Und die Blumlein schau' ich an,
Und die Aug'lein küss' ich dann:
Und der Mutter Herz vergisst,
Dass es draussen Frühling ist,
Dass es draussen Frühling ist,
Su, su, su, su! schlaf ein mein Kind.
Su, su, su, su!
In guter Ruh'!

The Image of the Rose.

(DAS BILD DER ROSE.)

G. REICHARDT.

Andante con espressione:

1. In yonder val - ley calm - ly bloom - ing, I saw a rose, its leaves un -
1. In ei - nem Tha - le fried - lich stil - le, Sah ei - ne Ro - se ich er -
2. And thus o'ercome with fond e - mo - tion I lin-ger'd, charm'd by this sweet
2. Und mich er - griff's mit süs - sem Be - ben be - zau - bert stand ich vor ihr
3. In dark and gloom - y hours of sad - ness, The form of that dear rose I
3. In trüb um - wölk - ten Trau - er - stun - den da zeigt sich mir der Ro - se

cres.

fold; Endow'd with sweet - er, brighter beau-ty Than I a - gain can e'er be - hold, By dew-y
steh'n; be-gabt mit ho - her, Schönheits Fül - le Wie ich noch kei - ne je ge - seh'n, In duf - tig
flow'r; From it my soul a joy re - ceiving, I ne'er had felt un - til that hour. Still in my
da; Es floss in mei - ne Brust ein Le - ben, wie nie auf Er - den mir ge - schah. Dies won-ne
sec, Then quickly grief gives place to gladness, And care and strife de - part from me. Yes, heav'n both
Bild, Und schnell ist Sorg' und Gram ver - schwunden, Und je - de Zäh - re ist ge - stillt. Was durch ver -

fra - grant moss sur - rounded, Shone forth the bud in full - est grace; A fairer em - blem than this
an - ge - schwell-tem Moo - se, Erschien der Knos - pe vol - le Pracht, Und schöner als in die - ser
in - most heart re - maineth, The cherished im - age of that rose, Und ever in the dis - tant
bild der Ro - se wei-let, In meiner treu - en, war - men Brust; Und in der fern - sten Zeit ent -
weal and woe de - cree-ing, Controls our life with se - cret pow'r To cheer my loneli - ness,
borg' - ner Mäch-te Wal - ten; Auf dunklen Pfa - den Licht er - schien; Soll Liebe treu im Bu - sen

più moto.

rose   Of holy vir - tue none shall trace,   A fair - er em - blem than this
Ro - se   Hat nie der Tu - gend Bild ge - lacht,   Und schöner als in die - ser
future   Shall its dear mem-'ry find re - pose,   And ev - er in tho dis - tant
ei - let,   Mir nie des Bil - des ew' - ge Lust,   Und in der fern - sten Zeit ent -
sorrow   To guide and bless me gave this flow'r,   To cheer my lone - - li - ness and
hal - ten,   Soll stets mit mir durch's Le - ben zieh'n,   Soll Lie - be treu im Bu - sen

piu moto: f

ten:

rose,   Of ho - ly vir - tue none shall trace,   Of ho - ly
Ro - se,   Hat nie der Tu - gend Bild ge - lacht,   Hat nie der
fu - ture   Shall it's dear mem' - ry find re - pose,   Shall its dear
ei - let,   Mir nie des Bil - des ew' - ge Lust,   Mir nie des
sor - row,   To guide and bless me gave this flow'r,   To guide and
hal - ten   Soll stets mit mir durch's Le - ben zieh'n,   Soll stets mit

cresp p

CODA. *Tempo Io molto espress.*

vir - tue none shall trace.   Im - age most dear,
Tu - gend Bild ge - lacht.   Lieb - li - ches Bild,
mem' - ry find re - pose.
Bild des ew' - ge Lust.
bless me gave this flow'r.
mir durch's Le - ben zieh'n.

p   *p*

pp

stay...... O stay......... O wei - le Stay O stay with me......
Wei - le, O wei - le Weile, O wei - le bei mir.................

mf   *p*

O YE TEARS! O YE TEARS!

Words by Dr. MACKAY.

Music by FRANZ ABT.

ANDANTINO.

PIANO. *mf*

2. O ye tears! O ye tears! as I felt ye on my cheek, I was

1. O ye tears! O ye tears! that have long re-fus'd to flow. Ye are

self - - ish in my sor - row; I was stub - - born, I was weak: Ye have

wel - - come to my heart, . . thawing, thaw - - ing like the snow; The

Con espress.

p

GERMANIA

giv'n me strength to con - - quer, and I stand e - rect and free, And
ice-bound clod has yield - ed, and the ear - - ly snow-drops spring, And the
know that I am hu - man, by the light of sym - pa - thy. O ye
heal - ing fountains gush, and the wilderness shall sing. O ye
tears! O ye tears!
tears! mf O ye tears!
5. There is light up - on my path! there is sun - - - - shine in my heart, And the
2. O ye tears! O ye tears! I am thank - - ful that ye run, Tho ye
4. O ye tears! O ye tears! ye re - lieve me of my pain, The
p
p

leaf   and fruit of life........   shall not ut - - - ter - ly de - part.   Ye r.

come   from cold and dark, ...   ye shall glit - - - ter in the sun ;
bar - - ren rock of pride........   has been strick - - en once a - gain ;   Like the

store to me   the fresh ness and the bloom   of long a - go,   O ye
rain-bow can - not cheer us if the show'rs re - fuse to fall,   And the
rock that Mo - - ses smote........   a - mid Ho - - reb's burn - ing sand,   It

tears!   O hap - py tears!   I am thankful that ye flow.   O ye
eyes   that can - not weep are the saddest eyes of all.   O ye
yields   the flow-ing wa - ter,   to make glad - ness in the land.   O ye

tears!   hap - py tears!

tears!   O ye tears!
tears!   O ye tears!

WE MEET ABOVE.

AUF WIEDERSEHN.

English words by J. S. DWIGHT.   LOUIS LIEBE. Op. 52.

1. Sun - shine,   clear and bright,   Floods all   my heart with light;   Warb - - ling with
1. Son-nen-licht,   Son - nen-schein   Fällt mir   ins Herz hin - ein.   Wie - - - ein Wald-

all its might,   No   bird   so blest!   For   now my pains are fled,
vö - ge-lein   Hüpft es   vor Lest;   Weil   es - sein Leid ver - gisst.

cres
Yes, now our souls are wed, Bliss - ful I lay my head . . . . Up-on thy
Weil du mein ei - gen bist, Weil du mich se - lich drückst . . . . . . An dei - ne
breast! Bliss - ful I lay my head Up-on thy breast!
Brust! Weil du mich se - - lich drückst An dei - ne Brust!
p rall.
colla voce.
2. Out in the morning dew,
3. In death, ere all is o'er,
2. Draus - sen auf grü - ner Au
3. Wenn ich einst ster - ben muss,
p mf
Blooms ma - - ny a blossom blue, Bloom - - eth, so sweet and true, For - get - me -
Ere yet my spir - it soar, Press . . . . . on my lips once more, Love's part - ing
Blü - hen viel Blümchen blau, Blü - - - hen Ver - giss - meinnicht, Bis man sie
Gieb mir zum Scheide - gruss Auf . . . . meinen bleichen Mund Den letz - - ten

legato.
cres.
not! Break them, they wither fast: But my true love shall last;
kiss! Gent - ly my eye-lids close, Pray for my soul's re - pose,
bricht; A - ber dann wel - ken sie, Nur mei - ne Lie - be nie,
Kuss. Druck mir die Au - gen zu, Wünsch' mir die ew' - ge Ruh,
marc.
Though break my heart at last, ... That with - ers not! Though break my
Say then: "We'll meet in bliss!" .... "We meet a - bove!" Say then: "We'll
Wenn auch das Her - ze bricht, ... Sie wel - ket nicht; Wenn auch das
Sa - ge: "auf Wie - der - sehn!" ...... "auf Wie - der sehn!" Sa - ge: "auf
p
rall.
heart at last, That with - ers not!
meet in bliss!" "We meet a - bove!"
Her - ze bricht, Sie wel - ket nicht!
Wie - der - sehn!" "auf Wie - der - sehn.
(Aug. Becker.)
colla voce.
p
mf
p

www.ingramcontent.com/pod-product-compliance
Lightning Source LLC
Chambersburg PA
CBHW030819270326
41928CB00007B/809